How To DOMINATE Your Market And Become The Go-To Listing Agent

Insider Secrets About How To Build A Predictable Real Estate Business With The Freedom To Enjoy It

ALEXANDER PIECH III

Copyright © 2018 Alexander Piech III All rights reserved.

This publication is licensed to the individual reader only. Duplication or distribution by any means, including email, disk, photocopy and recording, to a person other than the original purchaser is a violation of international copyright law.

Publisher: Alexander Piech

www.AlexPiech.com

While they have made every effort to verify the information here, neither the author nor the publisher assumes any responsibility for errors in, omissions from or different interpretation of the subject matter. This information may be subject to varying laws and practices in different areas, states and countries. The reader assumes all responsibility for use of the information.

The author and publisher shall in no event be held liable to any party for any damages arising directly or indirectly from any use of this material. Every effort has been made to accurately represent this product and its potential in their is no guarantee that you will earn any money using these techniques.

All rights reserved.
ISBN:
ISBN-13: 978-1979445948
ISBN-10: 197944594X

DEDICATION

This book is dedicated to my best friend and the love of my life, my wife, Sarah Piech. Your faith and constant support has given me the courage to take risks and pursue my dreams. I love you.

This book is also dedicated to my soon-to-be-born son, Nash. Finding out that I was going to be a father will always be one of the happiest days of my life. I want you to know that I will always be there to love you, support you, encourage you, and push you to think bigger.

CONTENTS

	Acknowledgments	vii
1	The Evolution Of Real Estate	Pg 1
2	Time Management Secrets Of The Most Successful Agents	Pg 13
3	How to Build a Predictable Pipeline	Pg 29
4	The Insider's Secrets To Generating A Consistent Flow Of Qualified Leads	Pg 43
5	Turning Leads Into Face-To-Face Appointments	Pg 59
6	How to Differentiate Yourself From The Competition So You Can List More Homes	Pg 69
7	Getting Started With Little To No Money	Pg 87
8	Why Choosing The Right Brokerage or Team Can Make All The Difference	Pg 107
9	The Success Strategy Plan	Pg 115

ACKNOWLEDGMENTS

There are a few people that I'd like to thank for helping make this book possible.

On the personal side I would like to thank my family, especially my mother and father who instilled in me an amazing work ethic. As a young child I watched my father bust his ass and work two jobs to support our family. I watched my mother go to work everyday and then come home take care of the house, cook dinner and help my brother and I with our school work. She never once complained. My parents have always supported, encouraged and believed in me.

If it wasn't for my father opening his first real estate office in 2003, this book and my real estate career would never have happened.

On the business side I would like to thank my mentor, Brian Moses. His impact on my business and personal development has been invaluable. Having been one of his coaching students for six years I was able to have personally experienced the impact that a coach can have in someone's life. That experience has led me to where I am today, it has ingrained in me a passion to contribute to others so that they can live an extraordinary life. I could never put into words how impactful his friendship has been.

INTRODUCTION

Hi, my name is Alex Piech, and I have been a licensed real estate agent since 2003. I was 20 years old and working a full-time job while also attending college full-time. It was at that time when my father decided to move his real estate brokerage out of our basement and into his first commercial location. I was in my second year of college and had no clue what I wanted to do after school so I decided to get my real estate license so I could help my father with his new office.

Within my first few months I had closed my first deal and I was hooked. After graduating college I wanted to focus on growing my real estate career. I partnered with my father and bought a RE/MAX franchise shortly after graduating and became one of the youngest franchise owners in their history, at the age of 22.

I quickly realized that the majority of agents only sold a few homes a year. I knew that there had to be a better way. I started researching top agents throughout the country and noticed that every top producer was following some type of coaching system.

I knew that if I wanted to reach my full potential I had to model what other successful agents were doing so I signed up for a three-day training seminar and flew to Denver. While I was there I signed up with my first real estate coach.

Even though I couldn't financially afford it, I knew that I couldn't afford not to hire a coach if I was serious about growing my business and reaching my goals.

Over the last 10 years, I have continued to invest in my personal and business growth. I have been obsessed with learning what systems and strategies produce the best results and have documented everything. I've taken the very best pieces of everything that I have learned and built systems and processes around these proven strategies.

This book is for any real estate agent who wants to build a predictable real estate business that generates a consistent six-figure income so that you never have to worry about where their next deal is coming from, never have to be concerned about paying their bills, never missing out on any of their kids' sporting events or worse, never feeling like they have failed and having to going back to a 9:00-to-5:00 job.

Let's get started…

Chapter 1

THE EVOLUTION OF REAL ESTATE

The Original Disrupter of Real Estate

In this chapter we are going to cover how real estate has changed over the last 20 years. We are going to cover the changes to the consumers search habits and how the Internet has created more competition and affected the ways that agents run their business.

Real estate dramatically changed in the late 1990s when a large number of local real estate boards throughout the country moved away from the biweekly printed Multiple Listing Service book (MLS) and moved to a web-based system.

Many of the original MLS systems ran off a DOS-based software system. At that time a computer would cost $2,500 to $3,000. Because of the high cost of owning a computer, many real estate boards continued to print MLS books for those agents who could not afford to buy a computer.

This advancement in technology would now allow Realtors

to do Keyword searches, allowing them to browse the inventory quicker and identify better properties based on their homebuyers' criteria.

In the early 2000s a browser-based system was created called the IDX (Internet Data Exchange). This would now allow the sharing of properties with individual websites.

Prior to the IDX and Internet, the Realtor was the gatekeeper of the information. Only Realtors had access to the inventory of homes for sale. Every two weeks a new MLS book would show up at their office with the updated homes for sale.

This meant that the consumer was completely reliant on the Realtor. Consumers had to drive to a local real estate office and meet with an agent to review the MLS book. Every two weeks when the newest edition would get delivered, the agent would search the book for any new listings that matched their homebuyers' criteria.

These books had hundreds to thousands of property listings, categorized by price. Which meant that the agent had to go through each listing by price point and then find the ones that matched their buyers' criteria. There was no way to search by the number of bedrooms, number of baths, square footage, acreage, style of home, or any other features and amenities.

With the MLS listings now being published online, the consumers' search habits start to shift. The consumer could now get access to a list of homes online without having to meet with a Realtor. The Realtor was no longer the gatekeeper of information.

Change in the Consumers' Search Habits

The Internet changed the consumers' search habits. Homebuyers could now get access to property details without having to meet face-to-face with a Realtor.

Not only did it change how homebuyers found property listings, it also changed how they found real estate agents.

With IDX making it possible to share properties through individual websites, the advent of companies such as Realtor.com, Zillow, and Trulia were born.

Over time IDX combined with improving technology made it possible for Realtors to have a fully functional MLS property search function within their personal websites.

Today, when you type the words "home search" into your Google browser, 249,000,000 search results are found within seconds.

Homebuyers could now get access to every home for sale in the country from the comfort of their own home. They now had access to all the details about each home, they could view color photos, and they could search by specific features that were important to them.

IDX Creates a Whole New Business

Websites like Realtor.com, Zillow, and Trulia started investing in consumer marketing. The race was on to win the consumer's eyes. In 2014 it was reported that Zillow was planning on spending $65 million in consumer advertising. Trulia was planning on spending $45 million.

Once these national platforms captured the attention and, more importantly, the eyes of the consumer, they began to capitalize on their website traffic by selling homebuyer leads to Realtors.

They were using the listings that Realtors provided them through the IDX agreements with the local MLSs and selling the homebuyer leads on those listings back to the Realtor.

Today it's not uncommon for Realtors to spend $1,000 to $25,000 or even $50,000 a month with these companies. They are considered to be the top lead-generation options for many Realtors today.

Marketing in the Internet Era

The change in the consumer search habits also created a change in the way that Realtors advertised.

If you go back 10, 15 years, every real estate agent and company was using the newspaper as the primary marketing platform. You could open up the Sunday real estate section and see pages of real estate ads. There would be small inline classified ads and display ads ranging from the size of a business card to full pages.

The top real estate companies would pay a premium for the back page of the newspaper, and they would commit to spending tens of thousands of dollars on these ads.

There were some major drawbacks to the newspaper ads:

- The picture quality was usually poor

- There was only one picture per property

- There was a limited amount of space to describe all the home's features

- The newspaper was only printed once a week

- Ads needed to be submitted several days before the publication was printed so properties could be one to two weeks old before they were advertised

In addition to the newspaper, home magazines were a

popular marketing option for many real estate companies and their agents. Home magazines also had many of the same drawbacks as the newspaper. None worse than the four to six weeks it took to print and publish the magazine.

Homebuyers were not getting relevant, real-time access to all the properties for sale with print marketing.

The Internet and IDX websites turned those newspaper and magazine drawbacks into advantages. IDX search sites have:

- High-quality photos of the property
- Display up to 36 pictures of each property
- Update with new properties daily
- Full HD video tours
- Aerial drone photos
- 3-D floor plans

Nowadays IDX websites are updating the list of available properties every 15 to 60 minutes allowing homebuyers to stay informed.

It's no wonder why 92+% of homebuyers today say they use the Internet during their home search and why the use of newspapers now only represents about 1% to 3% of their search. It's important to remember that a property's first impression happens online today. With the new 3D Video tours a buyer doesn't even need to ever walk through a house.

Today it is important for Realtors to have a strong online marketing presence. The good news is the cost of a robust website with IDX search built in has drastically dropped over the last 10 years.

IDX has also allowed Realtors to market their listings through every major platform, franchise website, and every agent's personal website exposing their seller's property to millions of potential homebuyers for nearly no cost.

At the time of writing this book, mobile advertising has already created another major shift with online marketing. Now it is vital that your online marketing platforms be mobile responsive because less and less consumer are using their computer to search online. They are using their cell phones.

Consumers are spending nearly one hour per day on social media sites, such as Facebook, Instagram, and YouTube. That has created new marketing opportunities for Realtors within these platforms.

Why the Best Agents Aren't the Ones Who Sell the Most Properties

With technology changing and major companies like Realtor.com, Zillow, and Trulia spending upwards of $65 million a year attracting consumers to their home search websites, it's become more expensive for Realtors to generate leads.

Realtors now have to learn an entire new set of skills. In addition to being a highly skilled Realtor, they need to learn and master the skill of digital marketing. They need to be able to consistently acquire new quality leads.

Online marketing is complex and can be difficult. To make things harder, every marketing platform is different and requires a unique understanding of how it works. Google Adwords is different from Facebook, and both are different than Instagram.

Even though online marketing has taken over as the primary source of marketing, the use of direct mail is still a very effective lead-generation tool. Direct mail can consist of postcards, letters, and three dimensional mail.

As with any marketing, your message plays a crucial part in your success. A great message that speaks to the needs of your ideal customer can dramatically increase the response rate.

It's my opinion that your ability to be an effective marketer has a direct correlation on how successful you are as a

Realtor. With marketing, the top producing Realtor isn't the one who is the most skilled or has the most knowledge; it's the Realtor with the best marketing who generates more quality leads.

More Competition Than Ever

With the advent of the Internet, competition has changed in the last 10 years. Realtors not only compete against other local agents, they now compete with agents from outside of their market. The IDX allowed agents to sell homes in any market. The agent didn't need to be the local expert or live in the area they serviced.

Now Realtors are also having to compete with large companies like Zillow, Opendoor, and OfferPad. These companies are disrupting the way real estate is being sold right now. These companies are now offering to buy homes directly from the homeowner without the involvement of a real estate agent.

These companies have built sophisticated home value algorithms that provide homeowners with their home's value in seconds. Consumers can go online, get their home's value, and request an instant cash offer. The consumer didn't need to worry about all of the stresses of selling a home. In addition, their fees are competitive to what a Realtor would charge the consumer.

Everyone Has a Real Estate License

According to the Association of Real Estate License Law Officials (ARELLO) there are 2 million real estate agents. As of April 2017, 1,236,544 were licensed Realtors according to the National Association of Realtors.

The main reason why there is such a large number of Realtors has to do with how easy it is to obtain a real estate license. The barrier of entry is so low that many people get a license as a hobby or part-time job.

According to the National Association of Realtors, the educational requirements to obtain a license is an average of 90 hours. Very often the educational requirements can be completed online. In addition to the low educational requirements, the cost of licensing is minimal.

Within three to eight weeks a person can get licensed as a Realtor. Licensed to represent somebody in the sale or purchase of their home, which is usually the largest financial asset that they own.

Just to put this into context, it takes 120 hours to get a CDL and become a truck driver, 600 hours to be a licensed nail technician, and 1500 hours to be a licensed beautician.

According to the National Association of Realtors, the average agent sold 5.8 homes in 2016. That's one home sale every other month. The lack of experience and expertise translated to a subpar consumer experience. So when the consumer or the public hears the word "Realtor," it's not synonymous with quality service, high standards, professionalism, honesty, and superior results.

As a result of so many people having a real estate license, competition is at an all-time high. Everyone knows someone with a license. They may have an aunt, a sister, mother, father, cousin, or a coworker who has a license.

When a large number of agents each do one or two transactions a year, that represents millions of transactions. That leaves full-time professionals competing for the remaining transactions.

Discount and Flat Fee Brokerages

Realtors have a new breed of agent coming into the market to compete against. They are called the discount agent. Anytime the real estate market is doing well and there is money to make, thousands of people jump into the business to make a quick buck.

When homes are selling quickly, discount agents come into the market, and the way that they get market share is to offer home sellers limited services but at a flat fee or reduced commission percentage.

The problem with being the cheapest is, in order to be the cheapest, something has to give. There has to be a compromise in the services provided to the consumer. What I've found is the consumer is left on their own to navigate the sale of their home.

Selling and buying a home is a very complex process so there is the opportunity to be sued at every single turn in the real estate transaction. By being left to manage the sale of their own home, the consumers take on a majority of the legal risk.

The challenge as a real estate professional is making sure you are armed and are educated to overcome that challenge when you meet with a home seller who says, "Why should I do business with you versus the guy who just walked out the door who said he would put my home on the market for $495?"

Later in the book I will cover how you can standout and differentiate yourself from the competition.

Now that you understand how the Internet has changed real estate and the consumer's search habits, we are going to go over the time management secrets that the top agents are using to outsell their competition.

Chapter 2

TIME MANAGEMENT SECRETS OF THE MOST SUCCESSFUL AGENTS

In this chapter we are going to go over the time management secrets that the most successful agents are using that allow them to outsell their competition.

Why the Most Successful Realtors Use a Calendar

Early in my real estate career, I was introduced to what I now consider one of the very best books ever written on business. The book was "The Ultimate Sales Machine" written by Chet Holmes. The very first chapter in the book is titled "Time Management Secrets of Billionaires."

The book lays out the framework that Chet Holmes used to take back control of his time while managing nine different business units and having 22 people directly reporting to him. In the book Chet goes through and breaks down six steps to great time management.

Understanding the value of time became very clear to me. The most successful people in the world still had the same

24 hours in the day and the same 7 days in a week. They were just spending their time more efficiently than everyone else. They understood how to organize and structure their time so they could be more productive.

In addition to Chet Holmes, I also studied the time management strategies of Darren Hardy, Dan Kennedy, and many of the top Realtors in the country. I took the core principles and adopted and modified them to the real estate business.

The first similarity I noticed was every successful person was using a calendar. They use calendars because it allows them to stay organized and adds structure to their day. Using a calendar lets them see quickly what commitments they have throughout the day. This structure allows them to be proactive versus reactive throughout the day.

In real estate, using a calendar to structure your time will add a sense of control into your business. At a glance you can see precisely what you should be doing. This helps ensure that you never miss anything important. It ensures that you never miss a follow-up phone call or show up late to an appointment because you got sidetracked doing something else.

The tool that I have found that works best is Google Calendar. Google Calendar syncs to all of your devices. It has pop-up notifications and reminder alerts. It allows for travel time in between appointments to make sure you never double-book yourself. You can also schedule meetings with people and have the meeting show up on their calendar with reminder notifications.

As a team leader or broker, having your agents use a calendar allows you to see what activities they are doing on a daily basis. You can see if their daily activities are aligned to achieving their goals. Not only is it a great productivity tool but it's a great accountability tool for your team.

The number one tip for better time management that I share with every agent, whether they are a single agent or a team lead, is to implement the use of a calendar.

Using Time Blocking to Accomplish More in Less Time

Time blocking is when you identify key times throughout the day and the week where you are going to work on a specific activity. I like to refer to it as doing deep work. This is uninterrupted scheduled time where you allocate 30 to 90 minutes to working on a specific project.

Time blocking allows you to prioritize and plan out projects or tasks that need to be completed by a certain time. Using dedicated time blocks helps prevent the last minute, night before panic where you have a project or task due that you haven't even started.

In real estate, that could be pulling the comps for a listing appointment in the morning. It could be submitting an offer before deadline for your buyer or sending over an inspection repair amendment before the deadline.

Many times in real estate agents have good intentions on building systems and processes in their business; however, they never get around to finishing these priorities. Maybe you want to build out a past client program to generate more referrals. You may have to spend some time thinking about it and maybe even started to write out some of the important pieces to implementing the program but never have been able to complete and implement the program.

Using the technique of time blocking would break down your project into smaller pieces and put time slots into your calendar over a period of time, allowing you to complete tasks. You will be shocked at how much you can accomplish in your business by setting aside dedicated time.

Using a Calendar to Grow Your Real Estate Business

One of the major benefits of using a calendar is aligning your time to the activities that help grow your business. Focus your time on the key areas of growth in your real estate business. I call these the high-dollar-producing activities.

In real estate, agents wear many hats. It's probably the thing that frustrates real estate agents the most. Agents feel like they have no time. They feel overwhelmed. This lack of control is a direct reflection of their calendar.

Earlier we spoke about how time blocking can allow you to take back control of your business. Now we are going to review what activities you should put into your calendar and help you prioritize those activities.

When prioritizing the activities, you will need to make sure that you are spending a majority of your time doing the highest dollar-per-hour activities. As a Realtor, there are three specific activities that generate the highest dollar-per-hour return.

Those activities are:

- Staying face-to-face with customers

- Prospecting for new customers

- Negotiating deals

There are no three activities in real estate that generate Realtors more money than those three. These activities are worth $250 to $500 an hour.

Don't believe me? Let me prove it to you.

Let's assume that you have a good quality listing; you've priced it correctly and marketed it correctly. The home sells for $300,000, and you receive a $9,000 commission check.

Now let's review how much time you spent working this listing.

- 1 Hour prepping for the listing appointment
- 1.5 Hours at the listing appointment
- 30 Minutes completing the listing paperwork
- 30 Minutes putting the listing in the MLS
- 2 Hours on marketing the home
- 1 Hour of market update call with the seller
- 1 Hour negotiating the offer
- 1 Hour negotiating inspection repairs
- 1 Hour managing the file up to the closing
- 1 Hour attending the closing

That's 10.5 hours of your time invested in this listing. You received $9,000 in commission. That's $857 per hour.

It becomes very clear why focusing on the three high dollar per-hour activities is vital to growing a profitable real estate business.

What we find most often is real estate agents are spending a majority of their time doing low dollar-per-hour activities, such as:

- Installing "For Sale" signs

- Putting a lockbox on the property

- Taking pictures of the property

- Filling the brochure box

Now, all those activities are required and necessary to do a good job in real estate, but those can be outsourced for $10 to $12 an hour.

In order to grow your business, you need to have an awareness of where you are spending your time. You need to limit the amount of time you spend doing low-dollar-productive activities and maximize the time you spend doing the highest-dollar-productive activities.

One of the ways you can do that is with time blocking. This

is where you lay out your calendar and block out time for those activities. In addition to the three primary activities we have talked about, there are other activities that should also be blocked out.

Here is a list of activities that should be time blocked in your calendar:

- Prospecting
- Face-to-Face Appointments
- Contract Presentations and Negotiation
- Training
- Marketing Review and Planning
- Community Events
- Email & Voice Mail Review
- Follow-up Phone Calls and Emails
- Date Night
- Family Activities

If you are like most people, you got into real estate for the flexibility. You quickly realized that the business could take over your life. It's important to have a good work-life balance.

As a free resource, here is a link to an example calendar.

BONUS DOWNLOAD
Download an example Google Calendar.
http://www.evolverealestatecoaching.com/example-calendar

As another free resource, I am going to share with you The Real Estate Nine Box. The Real Estate Nine Box breaks down all the functions in the real estate process . Each function has a written description of the job and a dollar-per-hour value associated with it.

BONUS DOWNLOAD
Download a free copy of the Real Estate Nine Box
http://www.evolverealestatecoaching.com/9-box

Why What You Do Today Affects Your Income in 90 Days

The challenge is real estate is not an instant gratification business. What I mean by that is we are not rewarded with a commission when we list a house. Realtors do not see the benefit of their efforts until the home has closed, which could be 45 to 120 days after they listed the home.

The opposite is also true that agents are not punished for bad behavior immediately either. What I mean by that is, if you miss a few prospecting time blocks each week, you don't feel any pain. You don't see or feel any change in your business immediately.

When agents are not disciplined to their calendar, they find themselves feeling overwhelmed. They are managing all the moving parts of every transaction, working 10-hour days seven days a week. While all of this is happening they usually can't find time to do the activities that generated the business in the first place.

They miss a few prospecting time blocks each week. They overlook their lead generation and marketing. Because these two vital activities get overlooked, no new business is being generated.

What's important to remember is sales happen in 60-to-120-day cycles. What you do or don't do today in your business is felt in 90 to 120 days. Those missed prospecting time blocks three months ago are now showing up in the form of an empty sales pipeline.

Now you are faced with an empty sales pipeline, and even if you buckle down and focus back on your lead generation and prospecting, those new leads will not turn to closing for another 60 to 90 days. This is what causes most Realtors to experience a yo-yo effect in their income.

Agents work hard, generate a bunch of business, and then they are so busy managing those transactions until they close that they don't bring in any new business. They close their deals and get paid and then go two months with no closings. They work hard again and generate more business, and the cycle goes on and on.

Proactive vs. Reactive

In real estate, it's easy to find yourself being very reactive. It happens every time your phone rings. A lead calls and asks to see a house, and you jump out of your seat and go show a home to a complete stranger.

One of the worst things that causes Realtors to be reactive is email. They are distracted every time an email pops up on their computer or their phone goes off and alerts them to a new email. Email creates a constant distraction.

Social media has quickly become a huge distraction for agents. What makes social media an even bigger distraction than email is the fact that every notification and pop-up is sent to your cell phone. The constant vibrating and pinging is almost irresistible to people. People have to look at their phone when they hear a notification. If you don't believe me, try. Try not looking at your phone next time it goes off.

The good news is you can easily use everything we have

reviewed on time management to be proactive. One of the ways you can be proactive is by putting designated time in your calendar for email review. Check email at 7:30am, 1:00pm, and 6:00pm. Allow 30 minutes in your calendar so you can review and respond to your emails.

This can also be done with voice mails. You can create a message that lets people know that you review your voice mails at 11:00am and again at 5:00pm. This will prevent people from calling you multiple times disrupting you, making you reactive. The other advantage to this is you set expectations on how you run your business. There is nothing worse than a client who expects you to be available 24/7.

The Secret to Using a To-Do List Correctly and How It Will Make You More Money

Most people use a list when they go grocery shopping or when they have errands to run. A to-do list should also be used in your real estate business. Using a to-do list will help you prioritize your daily activities.

Earlier in the book I laid out a list of activities that should be in your calendar. Those activities can also be included in your daily to-do list. I've taken the traditional to-do list and modified it for real estate.

In the real estate version of the to-do list, you write out all the activities that you have on your plate for the day and then prioritize those activities into A, B, or C priority.

A = Urgent Must-Dos

B = Important

C = Nice to Do but Not Required

In addition to prioritizing the activities, there is a section for a due date. This is where you set a completion deadline date for that activity. There is also a section for time. This is where you determine how much time you need to allocate to finishing the activity.

Finally, what makes this version of a to-do list so powerful is a value section. This is where you assign the dollar-per-hour value to that activity. By assigning a dollar value to the activity, you can evaluate how successful your day was.

People enjoy crossing items off their to-do list. It gives them a sense of accomplishment, which is why I encourage agents to use lists. However, if you had six items on your to-do list including getting face-to-face with a home seller, putting a lockbox on a property, taking pictures of a home, installing a for-sale sign, dropping off an escrow check, and creating brochures and you crossed off all except getting face-to-face with a seller which we identified as the highest dollar-per-hour activity, you need to seriously ask yourself,

"Did I win the day? Was I successful today?"

What I've found is most agents will cross off the easy-to-do, lowest dollar-productive activities to feel the sense of accomplishment, but they're not growing their business and they are not making more money. Using a to-do list will show you where you are spending the majority of your time and help you identify the important activities that will help you grow your business.

BONUS DOWNLOAD
Download a free copy of the real estate to-do list.
http://www.evolverealestatecoaching.com/to-do-list

Biggest Mistakes in Time Management

There are a few common mistakes I see Realtors make when it come to time management. The first and the biggest mistake is that they don't use a calendar. This entire chapter has been about the importance of using a calendar. If you have no structure in your day, I promise you will have no predictability in your business.

Other common mistakes are not creating repetitive tasks in their calendar that repeat each week. Agents plan one week at a time. What ends up happening is they have a busy weekend and don't get around to laying out their calendar for the coming week and end up being reactive throughout the week.

Agents should make certain activities repetitive week after week. Those activities should include the activities I laid out earlier in this chapter. Having recurring events happening on the same day and time every week provides clarity and certainty on what needs to be accomplished each week.

Another big mistake most Realtors make when it comes to time management is that they put the most important activities at the end of their day. For the average person willpower and energy are usually at their lowest at the end of the day. You have to do the hard things and the important things early, when you have the most energy.

There's a great book titled "Eat That Frog!" by Brain Tracy that's about the principle of doing the hard things first. Doing the hard things early in your day makes the rest of your day easy.

The last mistake I see is simply a lack of discipline to their calendar and doing the activities that they know they need to be doing.

Now that you know the secret time management techniques that the most successful agents are using to sell more homes, you can implement these strategies in your business and align your calendar to the activities that will allow you to take back control of your time and business.

Chapter 3

HOW TO BUILD A PREDICTABLE PIPELINE.

In this chapter we are going to cover a strategic system that if implemented in your real estate business will add a level of predictability to your sales pipeline helping you avoid the ups and downs and inconsistency in your transactions and income.

The Real Estate Roller Coaster

One of the biggest challenges real estate agents face is what is called the real estate roller coaster.

The roller coaster represents the up and downs, peaks and valleys in the real estate business. It represents the months when agents have multiple closings followed by the months when they have no closings and an empty sales pipeline.

For many agents the feast or famine cycle is endless. In Chapter 2, we touched on the primary reason agents experience volatility in their business. It's bad time management. Agents spend a majority of their time working on the wrong activities.

They do not focus on the most dollar-productive activities or revenue-generating activities because they get really busy managing their real estate transactions.

They are busy showing homes, writing contracts, negotiating contracts, attending home inspections, negotiating inspection repairs, and managing all of the mortgage contingencies.

They also have to manage the closing process with the title companies or attorneys. They do the final walk-through with their clients. Those are just a few steps. Each one of those steps goes layers and layers deep and the entire process can take 30 to 60 days.

Now multiply that workload by the three, four, five, or more clients that the agent is working with at any one time. When agents are handling all of these moving parts, they become so busy that they stop doing the activities that generated the business for them.

Those activities tie back to the three highest revenue-generating activities I wrote about in Chapter 2. They are prospecting for new opportunities, face-to-face appointments with new clients, and negotiating transactions.

After spending 30 to 60 days working on closing their transactions, the agent quickly realizes that their pipeline is now empty and they are starting back at zero.

They have to get busy and start generating leads again and start prospecting for new appointments. The challenge is even if they get another listing quickly it will be two months before they receive their next commission check. Real estate transactions can take 30 to 60 days on average to close. This is what causes the real estate roller coaster.

How Can I Get More Predictability with my Income?

Predictability is what many agents are chasing in their real estate business. The lack of predictability is what stresses out most agents and keeps them up at night.

One of the ways to get predictable income in your business is by building a strong sales pipeline. A pipeline is nothing more than a list of leads that you anticipate will become a client in the future.

The key to a predictable sales pipeline is identifying which of your leads has the highest probability of actually buying or selling a home. Once you identify those people, you need to create a Nurture process to continually build a relationship with that person so they want to do business with you. We call these prospects "Nurtures."

How do you identify who is most likely going to become a buyer or seller? You do this by asking a series of key questions to determine whether or not the prospect has a serious motivation and a specific time frame that they want their move to happen.

The Five Criteria of Identifying a Nurture

There are five criteria that a prospect must match in order to be classified as a Nurture lead. If the lead doesn't meet all five criteria, then they are not considered a Nurture lead and should not be added to your Nurture database. Adding leads that do not meet all five criteria will weaken the predictability of your pipeline.

Here are the five elements of a Nurture Lead:

1. The lead has a solid and identifiable motivation to make a move.

2. The lead has a clear time frame within the next 12 months.

3. The lead is not committed to another agent and is open to meeting with you.

4. You have valid contact information for future follow-up.

5. The lead provides you with a clear date to follow up with them.

1. The Lead Has a Solid and Identifiable Motivation to Make a Move.

This is your lead's why. Why are they considering making a move, and is it tied to a life event?

Example would be "I'm selling my house because we're downsizing once my child graduates high school in June."

2. The Lead Has a Clear Time Frame Within the Next 12 Months.

We use 12 months so that we can forecast what we expect our business to look like each year. If a lead has a time frame of more than 12 months, we put them in a long-term follow-up.

3. The Lead is Not Committed to Another Agent and is Open to Meeting with You.

The third criteria is that the customer is open to talking to you in the future about their real estate needs. Most of the time we're catching people early in the homebuying or selling process and they have not spoken to anyone else. We still want to confirm that they are not committed to another agent.

4. You Have Valid Contact Information for Future Follow-Up.

In order to stay in touch and Nurture the lead over the next 12 months, you need to have a valid phone number and email address. A cell phone is preferred so you can incorporate text messaging into your follow-up plan.

5. The Lead Provides You with a Clear Date to Follow Up with Them.

This date gives you a key nugget of information. It lets you know when the lead expects to get serious about buying or selling. It's an insight into their timeframe.

Why Nurtures are the Key to Predictability

A Nurture pipeline is an essential ingredient to creating a real estate business that predictably produces a consistent stream of transactions and commissions. Over time you will identify hundreds of Nurture leads.

Each Nurture lead will have their own specific follow-up date that they want you to follow up with them. This creates follow-up opportunities every month. Instead of searching for new leads each month, now you can focus on those who you have been building a relationship with.

Over time with the Nurture process, you will be able to have a more predictable income. You can make sales assumptions based on the conversion of your Nurture pipeline. You will be able to look at your Nurture pipeline and predict how many of your Nurtures will turn into a sale.

Many of your appointments will be with leads that you had previously spoken to and had in your Nurture pipeline. These Nurture leads will start to become more responsive to your follow-up and many times will reach out to you when they are ready to buy or sell.

This is when you start to get predictability in your business.

The Results Are In and The Nurture Process Works

When we implemented the Nurture process in the brokerage I was managing, we hit a tipping point where up to 50% of our monthly appointments were coming from Nurtures. We decided to take a deeper look in the Nurture process.

We had spent just over a year committed to building our Nurture database. We generated over 3,000 Nurtures, and now we wanted to see if Nurtures truly made a difference.

We decided to review every Nurture lead we identified from January 1, 2016 through July 31, 2016 to see how many of those leads actually turned into a transaction.

We pulled every seller Nurture from our database and cross-referenced their address in the MLS. The results were shocking. We identified that nearly 20% of the people that we identified as a Nurture lead had put their home on the market and had already sold their home.

If you have been in real estate for a while, you know that a 20% conversion on a lead source is unheard of. So when we uncovered that almost 20% of our Nurtures had not just listed their home but actually sold it, we knew that we were on to something special.

How Does Your Nurture Pipeline Stack Up?

It will be important for you to track your Nurture conversion to ensure that your Nurture pipeline is generating a consistent flow of opportunities.

You will want to scrub your Nurture list against the MLS sales quarterly. This will be essential in letting you know whether you are doing a good job qualifying your Nurture leads.

If you are not qualifying leads correctly with the five Nurture criteria, you will see a low conversion of your Nurtures. This means that you have allowed leads into your Nurture pipeline who do not meet ALL five criteria.

If you have done a great job identifying Nurtures and notice that your Nurtures are listing their home's for sale but with other agents, you have uncovered a breakdown in your Nurture follow-up process. We are going to cover in the next section the best practices of following up with your Nurture leads.

What Can I Do to Nurture and Follow Up with the Leads That I Get?

The key to following up is having a good customer relationship manager (CRM) that allows you to keep track of future follow-up tasks.

The most important task is the follow-up call. Your Nurture lead will give you a date to reach out to them. The rule of thumb we've all been told is to take that date and cut it in half. If a Nurture lead tells you to call them in six months, you need to call them in three months. It's always better to call too early than too late.

I would modify the frequency of the calls today based on the research and the actual results I've seen in the Nurture process. I would recommend a monthly call for anyone who is within six months and a call every-other-month for those who gave you a 6 to 12 months follow up date.

We also sent out handwritten thank you notes when we identify a Nurture. Another great way to stay in front of a

Nurture lead is to include them in your monthly mailings which can include your newsletter, market update reports, just listed and just sold postcards.

You can also mail client testimonials. Testimonials are effective because they provide social proof. They are a third-party validation and show that other buyers and sellers are having success doing business with you.

This is important because when you first speak to a new lead, they don't know you. Testimonials and property listing postcards allow you to validate why you are the best choice for them when it comes to buying or selling a home.

Today Realtors have a really big advantage. They have social media. They can go and search for their Nurture leads on LinkedIn, Facebook, and Instagram. Agents can use social media to gather important information about "who" their leads are.

Agents can invite their new Nurture leads to like their business page, which allows the lead to become more familiar with the agent. They get to learn who you are.

This is significant because people want to do business with people they know, like, and trust. This is a great opportunity for them to get a chance to know who you are.

What Are the Biggest Mistakes Agents Make When it Comes to Nurtures?

The biggest mistake agents make with the Nurture process is not qualifying the lead based on all five Nurture criteria. They include leads in their Nurture pipeline who only met a few of the criteria. They fill their Nurture pipeline with partially qualified leads.

Not only does this result in a lower conversion rate, but more importantly, it wastes valuable time following up with poor quality leads.

The second mistake is agents do not follow up enough. They allow too much time in between their follow-up activities. You need to stay top of mind with your leads. You need to show them that you are busy and getting results for others. You want to build trust and demonstrate value with your leads.

The third mistake agents make is they rely on technology alone to do the follow-up. They do not pick up the phone and call their leads. A quick call to just touch base is very effective.

These calls allow you to check in and see if anything has changed with your leads. Here is a simple script you can use:

Hi <Client First Name>, it's <Agent Name> with <Company Name>. How are things going?

Great, I just wanted to check in and see if you are still planning on making that move in <Time Frame>?

Sounds good. Is there anything in the meantime I can assist you with? Do you have any questions about the process or getting your home ready?

Okay, Well, let me know if there is anything you need from me.

The last mistake is agents are either not following an actual process or are inconstant in following the process.

What Will Nurtures Do for Your Business?

Nurtures will allow you to build a predictable real estate business. They will allow you to forecast your future income with certainty based on the conversion rate of your Nurture pipeline.

Nurtures can also help you double end more transactions. Because you have a list of future sellers who have expressed a serious interest in selling, you can use that database of sellers and cross-reference their homes features against the criteria of homebuyers you are working with.

You can also leverage your Nurture database to attract more buyers. You can let a potential buyer lead know that you have access to off-market listings. This is a great value to homebuyers, especially in a competitive market.

Now that you know how Nurture leads coupled with a well thought-out follow-up sequence can make your real estate business more predictable, we are going to cover the insider secrets to generating a consistent flow of quality leads.

Chapter 4

THE INSIDER'S SECRETS TO GENERATING A CONSISTENT FLOW OF QUALIFIED LEADS

One of the biggest complaints I hear from Realtors is that the leads they receive are poor-quality leads. In this chapter we are going to go over the process for identifying who your target leads are and the best way to attract them. We are also going to review the top five lead-generation strategies agents are using today to generate quality leads.

Who is Your Perfect Client?

When we talk about quality lead generation, it has to start with identifying who your ideal client is. We call this the process of identifying your Ideal Client Profile (ICP). This process forces you to think about the type of client that you would be excited to work with. Think of this as your dream client profile.

When creating your ICP, it's important to be specific and detailed. Some of the questions you want to answer when creating your ICP are:

- Is my ideal client a homebuyer, home seller, or a move-up buyer?

- What area are they looking to buy or sell in?

- What type of property are they buying or selling?

- What price range are they in?

- How much money are they putting down?

- How much equity do they have in their home?

- When do they want this move to happen?

The good news is that you can have more than one ICP. You may have one for buyers and one for sellers. Don't create multiple ICPs that are so opposite of each other that everyone could be considered an ideal client.

Ideal Client Profile for Homebuyers

Let's use the questions above to create an example of an ICP for a homebuyer.

My ideal client is a first-time homebuyer who is looking to purchase a home in Frisco or McKinney. They are looking for a single-family detached home with 3 bedrooms, 2 baths, a 2-car garage, between 1500 and 2200 square feet, and priced between $250,000 and $350,000. They are putting down 5% and want to be settled into their new home within 90 days.

The process of thinking through all the characteristics of your ideal client helps you get clear on what leads you should be spending your time with.

It also will help you with your marketing. We are going to dive deeper on using your ICP when creating your marketing later in this chapter.

Ideal Client Profile for Home Sellers

Let's use the questions above to create an example of an ICP for a home seller.

My ideal client is a homeowner who has a single-family detached home to sell in Frisco or McKinney that has equity in their property.

The home offers 3 bedrooms, 2 baths, a 2-car garage, between 1500 and 2200 square feet, and has a value between $250,000 and $350,000. The homeowner would like to have their home sold in the next 90 days.

Here Is A Bonus ICP. This Was My Favorite Client.

My ideal client is a move-up buyer who has a single-family detached home to sell in Frisco or McKinney. The home offers 3 bedrooms, 2 baths, a 2-car garage, between 1500 and 2200 square feet, and has a value between $250,000 and $350,000.

They want to buy a bigger home priced between $450,000 and $600,000. Their new home will be a minimum of 4 bedrooms, 3 baths, 3-car garage, and is 2500+ square feet.

They'll be using the equity from the sale of their current home to put down 20%. They would like to be situated in their new home within the next 90 days.

This was my favorite ICP because it represented two transactions with one client.

Understanding What Your Homebuyers Want

The key to working with a homebuyer is understanding what they want and what they value. There are the three things that are important to any homebuyer. Those three things are selection, affordability, and convenience.

When we talk about selection, we are talking about the number of homes available to our homebuyers. Selection for your homebuyer can also come in the form of the type of homes you provide to them. The type of selection can be new construction, coming-soon properties, and off-market listings.

The reason affordability is important to homebuyers is because every buyer wants to get a good deal. There are a few types of properties that homebuyers consider to be bargains.

By offering these types of homes to them, your services become more appealing and valuable. The type of homes include vacant homes, pre-foreclosures, bank-owned homes, and recent price reductions.

Convenience is how easy it is for the homebuyer to get access to the best selection of affordable homes.

Homebuyers want this information with the least amount of hassle. An easy way to offer convenience is to set your clients up in the MLS with auto notifications every time a home becomes available that meets or exceeds their criteria.

Now that you know the three things that are important to homebuyers, you can make sure that you use these hot buttons in your marketing to attract more motivated homebuyers.

Understanding What's Important to Home Sellers

The key to working with a home seller is understanding what they want and what they value. There are three things that are important to all home sellers. They are selling their home for top dollar, selling within a specific time frame, and having the least amount of hassle or sales pressure..

All sellers want to sell their home for the most amount of money possible. No one wants to leave money on the table. Your listings system should demonstrate how you can help drive up the demand on their home and ultimately give them the best chances at selling for the most amount of money.

Usually your clients have a specific time frame in mind when they want to have their home sold by. This time frame can be important to your homeowner.

It could be tied to a deadline, such as starting a new job or the start of a school year. Missing this deadline could cause your client lots of stress.

Your sellers want to be able to sell their home and do so with the least amount of hassle and sales pressure. As an agent, you can do a lot to help your seller have a good experience. You can set the proper expectations and explain the process to your sellers so they have comfort in the process.

Now that you know the three things that are important to home sellers, you can make sure that you use these hot buttons in your marketing to attract home sellers.

How Do I Attract My Ideal Client?

Now that you've taken time to clearly identify who your ideal client is, you can use all of that information and create marketing campaigns that will attract your ideal client.

When it comes to marketing, you attract your ideal client through your messaging. Your messaging is the words that you use in your advertising. Your message needs to resonate with your ideal client. It should be so strong that it causes a lead to respond and take the desired action that you tell them to.

Think of messaging like fishing. Your message is the bait or the lure you use to catch your fish. If we were going fishing for tuna, we would want bait that attracted tuna. If we were fishing for bass, we would want bait that attracted bass.

You want your messaging to attract the type of homebuyers and sellers that you want to work with. You also want your message to discourage other buyers and sellers who don't fit your ideal client persona not to respond to your marketing.

Creating a Buyer Message That Attracts Our ICP

Earlier, I provided an example buyer ICP. In that ICP I identified the areas of interest, price range, and property features that the buyer ICP would be interested in.

We can use that information and craft a message that would attract those homebuyers.

An example of a marketing message that would attract that specific buyer ICP would be:

****

Thinking about buying a home?

Get a FREE list of Frisco homes priced between $250,000 and $350,000

Visit: www.ExampleURL.com

****

10 Best Buys

Get a Free list of the 10 HOTTEST deals in Frisco

Priced between $250,000 and $350,000

Visit: www.ExampleURL.com

****

The key to these messages is they will only attract homebuyers who are interested in buying a home in Frisco and in are comfortable spending $250,000 to $350,000.

The ad will also eliminate homebuyers who are looking for homes priced below $250,000 and who are not interested in buying a home in Frisco.

Creating a Seller Message That Attracts Our ICP

Earlier, I provided an example homeowner ICP. With that ICP I identified the areas that I am interested in listing homes.

An example of a marketing message that would attract a seller who fits that ICP would be:

****

ATTENTION Frisco Homeowners

Thinking about selling your home?

Find out how much your Frisco home is worth.

Free Online Home Value Report

Visit: www.ExampleURL.com

****

The key to these messages is in the question, Thinking about selling? This allows us to identify those leads who are thinking about selling. It also speaks to Frisco homeowners only.

This ad would not attract homeowners who have a home outside of Frisco and those homeowners who are not interested in selling.

Understanding how important the role of messaging is in lead generation is critical in how effective your ads will be and the quality of lead you attract.

Before you run another ad, look at your message and ask yourself, "Does my message appeal to the type of buyer or seller that I'm excited about doing business with?"

If it does not, then rewrite the ad using some of the important qualifiers that you identified when you created your ICP.

Where's the Best Place to Generate Leads?

Now that you have your marketing message dialed in, you need to find the right media to run your ad in. You have a lot of options today. There's a bunch of different media to place your ads.

We've broken those down into three different types of

media. Those media options are expensive, inexpensive, and free media.

Expensive media can be classified as any type of media that cost more than $1,000 a month. They can be radio, TV, billboards, Zillow, park benches, or shopping carts.

Inexpensive media is anything that cost less than $1,000 a month. Examples of inexpensive media can be Facebook or Google Pay per click if they are done right. When these are done correctly, you can generate leads for as little as a few dollars per lead.

Free media cost you nothing. Free media can include Craigslist, for sale sign, sign riders, business card, property brochures, and much, much more.

Make sure that you're taking advantage of all the free and inexpensive opportunities available to you in your market. You need to get all the meat off the bone.

The combination of having the right message and using the right media to deliver that message will help you generate a consistent flow of qualified leads.

In Chapter 7, we're going to discuss all the free types of lead-generation opportunities to help you get started with little to no money.

The Top Five Lead-Generation Strategies Every Top Producing Agent Uses in Their Business

When it comes to marketing in real estate, there are millions of options. If you search the words "Real Estate" in Google, you'll find over 918 million websites. There's also no shortage of companies trying to sell you leads.

There are five staple lead-generation and marketing strategies that every single top producer has set up in their real estate business.

Expired Leads

I'm not going to spend a lot of time on expired leads in this chapter. There will be an entire section in Chapter 7 where I go deep into expired lead opportunities and best practices on how to convert them.

I will say that the reason why expired leads are a part of every top agent's lead-generation strategy and why it should also be one of your top strategies is because the homeowner has already identified themselves as somebody who wants to sell their home.

Seller Home Evaluation Leads

A home evaluation lead is a seller who responded to your ad and has requested to find out how much their home is worth.

The reason this is a core strategy for top producers is because it attracts listing leads. Every top agent understands that they need to list to last in this business.

Homeowners will exchange their contact information and provide details about their home in order to get an idea of what their home is worth in the current market.

Using some of the marketing techniques we discussed earlier in this chapter can generate seller leads for as little as $5 to $10 a lead.

For Sale By Owner Leads

I'm not going to spend a lot of time on FSBO leads in this chapter. There will be an entire section in Chapter 7 where I go deep into FSBO lead opportunities and best practices on how to convert them.

FSBO leads are similar to expired leads in that the homeowner has already identified themselves as somebody who wants to sell their home; however, FSBO leads offer agents even more valuable information such as how much they think their home is worth because they put a price in their advertising.

Repeat and Referral Leads

Research shows that it cost 5-10 times more to acquire a new customer than it does to retain an existing customer. As I'm sure you already know, marketing and lead generation can be expensive. For that reason the top agents build strong repeat and referral databases.

These top agents build systems around their database of past clients. Their systems are designed to communicate with their best clients, keep their clients informed about the market, and strengthen their relationship.

This investment into the relationship results in their past clients sending them referrals and results in clients coming back to the agent for repeat business.

The top agents in the country account for 30% or more of their business coming from repeat and referral leads.

Open House Leads

I'm not going to spend a lot of time on open house leads in this chapter. There will be an entire section in Chapter 7 where I go deep into open house lead opportunities and best practices on how to convert them.

I will tell you this; that the strategy we talk about in Chapter 7 is not your traditional open house where the only visitors are the nosey neighbors.

BONUS

Event-Based Prospecting

There is a bonus strategy that I wanted to include in the book, and that is event-based prospecting. Event-based prospecting means that anytime an event has happened around a home, we circle prospect the neighbors.

The different types of events that you want to leverage in this strategy are:

- When a home is Just Listed

- When you are doing an Open House

- When a home changes to Pending status

- When a home is Sold

When any of these things happen around one of your listings, there is an opportunity for you to reach out to the neighbors. I want you to think about these as opportunities to create brand impressions with each neighbor.

When you list a home and put a for sale sign in the ground, you are creating an impression every time a neighbor drives by the home. When you make the four event-based calls to the neighbors, you are creating more impressions.

You are letting the neighbors know who you are and that you are a hardworking agent who is getting results for their neighbor.

The beauty to this strategy is not only will it generate more listing opportunities for you, but the listing will be in the same neighborhood where you have already done business.

This is one of the secret strategies that top agents are using to gain massive market share and become the dominate go-to agent neighborhood by neighborhood.

BONUS DOWNLOAD
Download a free copy of my event-based dialing script
http://www.evolverealestatecoaching.com/event-based-scripts

Now that you know the secrets that the top agents are using to generate a consistent stream of quality leads, in the next chapter we are going to cover the best strategies to convert your leads to appointments.

Chapter 5

TURNING LEADS INTO FACE-TO-FACE APPOINTMENTS

In this chapter we're going to go over the process on how to set more face-to-face appointments using a five-step method that will allow you to convert leads. We are also going to review the qualifying process to ensure that the appointments you set are quality appointments.

Five Steps to Converting Leads to Face-To-Face Appointment

When it comes to building a successful real estate business, you should leave nothing to chance. We've already discussed in the previous chapter the cost of generating leads. If you're going to spend money on generating leads, it's important that you have a process to convert those leads into appointments. Here is the five critical steps on how to convert more of your leads into face-to-face appointments.

Step 1: Calling Your Leads

I know that this sounds elementary; however, you would be shocked at the number of leads that never get called.

The most important factor when it comes to calling leads is your speed of response. According to the MIT Lead Response Management Study, speed of response plays the biggest role in being able to reach and convert a lead into a face-to-face appointment.

In the MIT study, they found that responding to a lead within the first five minutes produced the highest probability of turning that lead into an appointment.

The study showed that you are 100 times less likely to reach a lead if you called them 30 minutes after they register versus calling them in the first 5 minutes.

In addition to calling your leads quickly, another important approach is to call often. You should make multiple attempts to call your leads. In a recent study they found that it takes an average of 12 call attempts to actually reach and connect with an online lead. Here are some best practices:

On Day 1 you need to make at least three call attempts. Stagger your calls throughout the day. Try a call early in the morning, middle of the afternoon, and later in the evening.

On Day 2 through 7, make at least one call attempt per day. After the first week you should attempt to call two to three times each week for the next three weeks. This process will ensure that you have made at least 15 call attempts and have given yourself the best odds to reach your leads.

It's helpful to have a contact relationship manager (CRM) that will keep track of your call attempts and will let you sort your leads by the number of attempted calls.

Step 2: Reaching Your Leads

If you can't reach your leads, you'll never be able to set appointments. I refer to this as your spoke-to rate. This conversion metric is one of the most important metrics in your entire business. This single metric can predict the success or lack thereof that you will have in your business.

There are a few important strategies that will allow you to increase the number of leads that you reach. One of those strategies is the days in which you call your leads, and the other is the time of day that you call your leads.

In the MIT study, they tracked and measured which days and times of day produced the highest spoke to and conversion rate.

Best Time To Call Your Leads

The study found that the best times of the day to make calls were between 4:00pm and 6:00pm and between 8:00am and 9:00am. Because the study was tracking corporate businesses, they did not include calls after 6:00pm.

In my personal business and in the businesses of those agents who I have worked with over the years, I have found that calling between the hours of 7:00pm and 9:00pm is also very effective.

When you take a look at the time frames in the MIT study, you can see why certain times of the day are better that others. Early morning calls between 8:00am and 9:00am allow you to reach your leads before they start their workday.

Evening calling between 4:00pm and 6:00pm, which was found to be the best time to call leads, does make perfect sense because your leads are usually finished with their workday by this time.

When it comes to real estate, what I found is that 7:00pm to 9:00pm may be an even better time to reach your leads. By this time your leads are usually home for the night. This gives you a great opportunity to reach your leads.

Best Days to Call Leads

Now let's take a look at the best day to reach your leads according to the MIT study. The MIT study reveals that Wednesday and Thursday are the best days to get in touch with contacts. They were 49.7% more effective than the worst days to reach and contact people.

Again, because the MIT study was done with corporate businesses, they only tracked calls made Monday through Friday. What I have found over the years is that Saturday mornings are also a great day to reach leads.

What Do You Do with This Information?

In Chapter 1 we talked about the importance of time management. Now that you know which days and times give you the highest probability to reach your leads, you need to time block you calendar accordingly. Every market is different so you can test the days and times to see what produces more results in your business.

Tips to Help Improve
the Number of Leads You Reach

Here are a few tips and tricks that I have found over the years.

Try calling your leads from a different phone number. If you have made a few calls with no luck, try switching up the number you call from. Try calling once from your office phone and then again from your cell phone.

Try calling back to back. If you call your lead and no one answers, hang up and call back. You can even do this a third time. By calling back to back, you create a level of curiosity in the prospect's mind. They immediately start to think that the call must be important.

Do not leave a voice mail for the first three days. Once you leave a voice mail, the prospect knows that you are a real estate agent and they know which number you are calling from. In 14+ years I've never met an agent who successfully got leads to call them back from voice mails.

Step 3: Make a Compelling Offer

A compelling offer is an offer that provides value to the prospect. The offer has to be good enough that it makes the prospect want to meet with you.

Your compelling offer has to answer this question for the prospect: "What's in it for me?" What problem are you solving for the prospect? Keep in mind that homebuyers and sellers each have a unique set of problems.

In order to make homebuyers a compelling offer, you first need to understand what's important to them. There are three essentials that all buyers want when it comes to buying a home. They are selection, affordability, and convenience.

In order to make a seller a compelling offer, you first need to understand what's important to them. There are three essentials that all sellers want when it comes to selling their home. They are getting top dollar, selling within a specific time frame, and no sales pressure.

Step 4: Handle Common Objections

Being able to handle common objections is one of the most important steps in converting leads to face-to-face appointments.

The good news is there are only a handful of objections that a homebuyer and home seller have. Taking note of the most common objections and crafting rebuttals that overcome these objections is crucial to setting more appointments.

An article published by CoolLifeCRM outlined various research studies done on conversion. It identified that 44% of sales professionals give up after the customer said no to their offer one time, 22% gave up after the customer said no two times, 14% gave up after the customer said no three times, 12% gave up after the customer said no four times. That equals 92% of sales professionals who give up after they've been told no four times.

Now, when you compare that to the customer's behavior, you may be shocked to learn that 80% of prospects say no four times before they say yes. The study showcased why 8% of sales professionals are doing 80% of the business.

Step 5: Qualifying the Lead

Now that you have set the appointment, it's time to qualify that lead. The qualifying process is important because you do not want to waste time on unqualified people.

Qualifying is where you determine if you want to keep the appointment or cancel the appointment. When you qualify a lead, you want to ask a series of questions that determines the prospect's timing and motivation for doing business.

Based on how the prospect answers these qualifying questions, you can either move forward with the appointment or cancel the appointment.

BONUS DOWNLOAD
Get access to our list of qualifying questions
http://www.evolverealestatecoaching.com/qualifying-questions

Why Using Scripts Results in More Appointments

Why are scripts important? Scripts are important because they provide you a framework for the conversations that you have with your customers. They allow you to stay in control of the conversation and move your prospect closer to making a buying decision.

Having a script ensures that you never skip over anything important. It will allow you to articulate your value proposition the exact same way every time. This is important because it systemizes your business and makes it more predictable.

A well-written script should include the three elements we discussed earlier. For buyers your script should offer selection, affordability, and convenience to the prospects. Scripts also can give you more confidence to convert any type of lead.

Biggest Mistakes People Make When it Comes to Prospecting Leads

The biggest mistakes I've seen real estate agents make is not using a script or not following the script.

When an agent doesn't use a script, they are at risk of forgetting or skipping important elements of their value proposition, which reduces the likelihood of setting face-to-face appointments.

When agents do not use a script, they're not following a process. Without a process they have no way to determine what's working and what needs to improve.

Another major mistake that I see is when agents qualify leads before adding value. They start by asking a lot of personal questions. These questions are self-serving and add no value to the prospect.

Agents ask questions about the prospect's timing, their motivation, their financial ability to purchase a home, how much money they have, how much they're putting down, and their time frame for buying a home.

Now, all these are good questions, but when they're asked prior to adding value and building a relationship with the prospect, they cause friction. The prospect does not know you, they do not trust you, and when you ask this level of question, you are instantly out of rapport with the client.

Another mistake I see is when agents do not have a value proposition for why the client needs to do business with them over any of the competition. They cannot communicate their differentiation over the phone or make a compelling reason as to why the prospect should meet with them.

Now that we have covered the five steps to convert leads into face-to-face appointments, we will review the best techniques to convert those leads into customers by differentiating yourself from the competition in the next chapter.

Chapter 6

HOW TO DIFFERENTIATE YOURSELF FROM THE COMPETITION SO YOU CAN LIST MORE HOMES

In this chapter we will cover the variety of ways that you can differentiate yourself from the competition so that you can win more listings at the right price.

Why Do You Need to Differentiate Yourself?

One of the most important things that you can do as a real estate professional is to differentiate yourself and your services from the average real estate agent in your market. The reason differentiation is so important is because in the consumer's mind, all real estate agents are the same.

The consumer doesn't see a difference in the quality of the real estate agent or the services that they provide. Because the consumer doesn't see a value in the agent or their services, the agent is viewed as a commodity.

When there is a lack of differentiated value, the consumer will select an agent based on who will charge the lowest commission or who's willing to list the property at the highest price.

An example of this is when the consumer decides to list their home for sale by owner. The consumer sees so little value in the real estate agent that they believe that they can sell their own home without the assistance of a Realtor.

They don't see the value in paying a real estate agent their commission and many times believe that they can net more money if they sell their home on their own.

It is imperative that you differentiate yourself and your services in a way that adds value to the consumer. When you have a defining value proposition where the consumer sees so much value in your services, they no longer base their decision on your fee.

Using Data to Become an Expert

One of the best ways to differentiate yourself when you're face-to-face with a customer is by using market data. When you use market data, you position yourself as an expert, somebody who is up to speed on the market and someone who is knowledgeable.

What Data Should You Use When You're Meeting with Customers Face-To-Face?

When you're meeting with a customer and you're using data to position yourself as an expert and somebody who is knowledgeable about the market, the following data information should be used:

Current Active Data: The current active data will show the homeowner(s) what homes they will be competing with when they go on the market.

Current Pending Data: The current pending data will display which homes have recently attracted an offer. This helps identify what the current buyers in the market are interested in. The pending ratio is also an important indicator as to how active the market is.

Past Six Month Expired Data: The past six month expired data is important because it can identify any trends that are causing homes to fail to sell.

Past Six Month Closed Data: The past six month closed data is important because it provides additional data that is critical such as:

- List Price to Sales Price Ratio
- Average Days on Market
- Absorption Rate
- Months Supply of Inventory

One of the most important pieces of data that should be used by real estate agents is the absorption rate. The absorption rate compares the average number of homes selling each month to the number of active homes on the market. This gives you the month's supply of inventory.

Understanding the month's supply of inventory is an important piece of information when it comes to pricing a home properly. There are three types of markets that can be identified using this data.

The first is a normal market. A normal market is a market that has five months' supply of inventory. A normal market represents a market that has price appreciation, which is in alignment with the historical norms of 2 1/2 to 3 1/2% annually growth.

The second market is a seller's market. A seller's market is a market that has less than five months' supply of inventory. This means that there are more buyers buying homes than there is inventory to choose from. In a seller's market prices are appreciating faster. In past sellers markets price appreciation has been 4 to 10% or higher annual growth.

The third market is a buyer's market. A buyer's market is a market that has more than five months' supply of inventory. This means that there are more homes for sale than there are buyers buying. In a buyer's market prices are slowing or in some cases depreciating.

Getting access to this information is getting easier. When I first started selling real estate, I had to spend hours every month compiling information from my MLS and creating spreadsheets with complex mathematical formulas to get this information.

Nowadays you can get this data quickly and inexpensively. One of the best services that I used in business was a monthly national real estate market update from Keeping Current Matters. For $20 a month they provided a monthly webinar with PowerPoint slides that I could use in my listing presentation. Their monthly market update kept me informed on all the critical real estate trends.

By leveraging this technology I instantly demonstrated my expertise and built credibility with the customer.

Another service that I used in my real estate business was local market reports by Real Market Reports. These local reports provided me data at the city and ZIP Code level. You can think of Keeping Current Matters as the 30,000-foot view of the overall real estate economy and Real Market Reports as the 10,000-foot view over the city.

Real Market Reports provide great information, from the number of active homes, the current pending ratios, which price ranges are selling at the highest level, which price ranges are attracting the most buyers, which price ranges are expiring and failing to sell, and the average days on market.

They also produce graphical information that visualizes all of this data that makes it easy to understand for the homeowners.

Real Market Reports also breaks the market down by price bracket, which helps you do a better job at evaluating the proper price strategy for your listing. Each price bracket has the current active inventory data, current pending, inventory data, expired data, closed data, and the month's supply of inventory by price bracket.

Having this data allows me to stand out amongst my competition. Over the years I have asked hundreds of homeowners if any of the other agents shared this information with them. In 14+ years, no one had ever said yes. By educating sellers and showing them the market data I instantly differentiated myself and demonstrated my expertise.

Providing Services That Add Value to Your Seller Clients That Create a WOW Experience

One of the ways that you can differentiate yourself is by showing homeowners how you're going to position their home so that it stands out against all the other competing homes in the market.

One of the absolute best ways to do this is by professional staging. Homes that are professionally staged, according to market research, will sell for up to 17% more money. These staged homes also sell 72% faster than other homes that are not staged.

Market research shows that a 1% investment in staging can return up to 1000% ROI, return on investment. Staging is extremely important for a few reasons. Number one, a professional stager can showcase a room's features and visual aspects.

Number two, most people, when touring a home, have difficulty imagining how to position furniture. A professionally staged home can allow somebody with a lack of imagination to instantly see how a home could work for them and see what type of furniture fits the space and design of the home.

There are many options when it comes to staging. In my business we used a two-hour touch-up plan. Our stagers would use the homeowner's furniture to stage the home. They would help declutter and make small recommendations to the owners. This service cost less than $300 per listing.

Another service that can help your seller's home stand out amongst competition is a pre-inspection. The reason this is so important is the home inspection is the number one deal-killer in real estate. In a traditional real estate transaction, a buyer makes an offer. They negotiate with the seller, and they settle on a price. After the offer is accepted the buyer will do a home inspection. Because no home is perfect, the buyer usually comes back to the seller and wants to renegotiate on repairs. Sometimes the buyer finds items that are so costly or important that the buyer actually withdraws their offer.

By getting a pre-inspection, we can identify in advance any potential deal-killers that might arise. We can also identify some common wear and tear and repairs that our home seller can actually take care of before putting the home on the market.

By identifying these repairs before the home is on the market, the home seller can do some of the repairs themselves or can hire a professional in that field and get the repairs done. This is significant because homebuyers will request that a licensed contractor do all repairs if they uncover the issue during their inspection. This can increase the cost of the repairs for your sellers.

By having a pre-inspection done on a home, you put your sellers in a position of strength when it comes to negotiation. When a buyer comes to one of my listings, I provide them with a full home inspection that was done on the property. I can provide them with receipts for the repairs that my sellers have already taken care of. This reduces the buyer's negotiating power.

By having a pre-inspection done, our homeowners also benefit because it reduces their liability when it comes to disclosure. Most sellers are not professional contractors; therefore, making statements about their home's condition can sometimes lead to legal issues. By providing a professional inspection to the homebuyer, they reduce their liability.

Another service that you can use to help your listings stand out amongst the competition is a home warranty. Warranties are useful for a few reasons. They can provide sellers protection during the listing period and offer peace of mind to the buyer after they purchase the home.

Most agents aren't aware of this, but certain home warranty companies provide seller coverage absolutely free. They protect the seller and cover most of the major mechanicals while the home is actively being sold. If the seller has any issues arise while the home is active, they can call the warranty company and for a small service fee between $75 and $100, the warranty company will take care of the repairs, saving your sellers thousands of dollars on potential repairs.

Home warranties also provide potential buyers an extended one-year coverage plan. This protects them from unforeseen major mechanical defects. It gives homebuyers peace of mind. Market research shows that a property that offers a warranty will sell for between 2% and 2.2% more money.

The Strategy of Maximum Exposure

Being able to show your seller a strategy on how to drive up the demand on their home and attract buyers that are willing to pay top dollar will set you apart from your competition.

Using a written marketing plan in your listing presentation that clearly outlines your marketing strategies will assist you in articulating your value to a home seller. This marketing plan shows the sellers how you plan to allocate your marketing budget and tells them where you're going to invest in advertising.

In today's world, the Internet is vital when it comes to being able to sell a home. Market research shows that 92% of buyers are using the Internet during their homebuying process. This comes from the National Association of Realtor's 2016 homebuyer-home seller survey.

Your marketing plan will need to include an online strategy that focuses on the main search sites where homebuyers are actively searching for homes. Those search platforms are Google, Yahoo, and Bing. These three platforms make up 99% of all homebuyer search traffic.

In addition to knowing the top search platforms, you need

to know the top five websites customers are using to search for homes. The top five websites are Zillow, Trulia, realtor.com, Yahoo Real Estate, and homes.com.

Showing your home seller that you know where buyers are looking for homes and that you have a marketing plan that includes these medias will demonstrate your marketing knowledge.

Because 92% of buyers are using the Internet in their home search, the quality of your photos is critical. You will want to use a professional photographer for all of your listings. The reason professional photography is important is because the first showing on a home is no longer when the buyer walks in the door; the first showing happens online.

You need to make sure that you are using a professional photographer who specializes in real estate and who has the proper equipment. You want to be able to show your sellers pictures that you've done on other properties, and it also helps to show them the difference between great photos and average photos. Check your MLS. I'm sure you can find photos taken by agents using their iPhones.

In addition to photography, you also want to use virtual tours, HD video walk-throughs, 3-D dollhouse tours, and drone footage. All of these are ways of exposing and showcasing the home's features. These media have become more important with the growth of the Internet.

Do You Know About the Three Types of Homebuyers?

Another way that you can differentiate yourself from your competition is by informing your seller of marketing strategies that they've never heard of or that other real estate agents are not talking about.

An example of this is asking your home sellers if they are aware of the three types of homebuyers or asking them if any of the other agents they interviewed talked about the three types of homebuyers. In 14+ years I have never had a seller say that another agent mentioned the three types of homebuyers.

The three types of homebuyers are the in-town buyers, the out-of-town buyers, and the buyers who are working with another agent.

Now that you have peaked your sellers' interest about the three types of buyers, you can demonstrate how your unique marketing strategy attracts each type of buyer.

The key to this strategy is to inform your sellers that over 71% of homes are sold with two different real estate companies. This means that the largest pool of buyers is actually already working with another agent.

You can use this data to make your services more valuable

to the sellers by having a strategy to market their home to a cooperating agent. Again, this will be a unique marketing strategy that other agents didn't review with the sellers. This will differentiate you from your competition.

Your strategy to expose their home can include targeting buyer specialists or top agents in your market and informing them about your new listing prior to it going into the MLS. This will help increase the showings from cooperating agents and allow your seller's home to stay top of mind with these top agents.

Another way you can entice cooperating agents is through commission leverage. Offering a competitive co-broker fee or even offering a high compensation or bonus can cause agents to push their buyers to viewing your listing before the competition.

One of the biggest mistakes homeowners make is that they want to reduce the real estate commission. The problem with reducing the real estate commission is many times that reduction in the commission is reflected in the cooperating commission that is being paid out to the buyer agent.

The threat to reducing the co-broker fee is that is it makes your property less desirable for the agent to show. It could cause buyer agents to push their homebuyers to other properties.

With almost 3 out of 4 buyers working with another agent, your seller can not afford to limit their homes appeal to that large a group of buyers. This will cause their home to take longer to sell and will cause the home not to attract the highest offer.

Some of the ways that you can attract homebuyers is through buyer incentives. Buyer incentives make buying one home more attractive than its competition. Buyer incentives can include assistance with closing costs, repair allowances, offering a home warranty for the buyer, and an interest rate buy-down.

Creating a Buzz About Your Listing

Now that you have implanted the strategies I have laid out in this chapter and won the listing, you need to start the marketing process. While your sellers are getting their home prepared, you can utilize a marketing strategy called the coming-soon process.

The coming-soon process is a premarketing strategy where you put a coming-soon sign in the yard 7 to 10 days before the home goes live in the MLS. This will allow you to start fielding inbound sign calls and inquiries about your listings.

You can use this time to notify the top agents in the market about your new listing. You can also reach out to your database of homebuyers and notify them of your new listing.

The coming-soon strategy allows you to increase the buyer interest in your property, which creates a buzz so the first day that your new listing becomes active on the market, you get a high volume of showings. This strategy sometimes can result in multiple offers.

Utilizing the coming-soon process will also allow you to build a buyer-in-waiting program which allows you to match your existing buyers to your coming-soon listing and double-end more listings.

Unique Selling Proposition

One of the absolute best ways to differentiate yourself amongst your competition is to offer a unique selling proposition. A unique selling proposition or position is a service that you offer that your competition does not.

Dan Kennedy says a USP should answer the question of why a customer should do business with you versus doing business with your competition or choosing to do nothing at all.

An example of a unique selling proposition that attracts sellers is:

Your Home SOLD in 59 days Guaranteed or I'll buy it for cash.

An example of a unique selling proposition that attracts buyers is:

If you're not satisfied with the home you buy, we'll sell it for free.

USPs allow you to stand out in your marketplace. They also are a very good marketing strategy that procures lots of consumer interest.

Performance Guarantees

Performance guarantees are also an effective way to differentiate yourself. A performance guarantee can reduce the risk of doing business with you. They can guarantee a specific result for your customer and add a level of accountability to your services.

Some good performance guarantees that you can use in your business are a satisfaction guarantee or a cancellation guarantee. This guarantee allows your customer to end their relationship with you at any time if they are not 100% happy with your services.

An additional performance guarantee you can use for homebuyers is a guaranteed saving. This guarantee states that you will save your client a specific amount of money off the purchase price of the home they choose or you will provide them something in exchange, such as a credit for closing costs.

A performance guarantee you can offer to sellers is a communication guarantee. This is significant because according to the NAR survey, 68% of consumers were dissatisfied with the lack of communication with their real estate agent.

A communication guarantee can assure your client that you will communicate with them consistently or you will provide them something in exchange, such as a credit for closing costs.

To make your performance guarantees more substantial, you should have them in writing. This makes your claims more believable.

Now that we have covered the importance of differentiation along with a variety of ways to add value to your customers so they can sell their home for the most amount of money, we will cover how you can get started with little to no money.

Chapter 7

GETTING STARTED WITH LITTLE TO NO MONEY

In this chapter we are going to break down free and inexpensive lead-generation strategies that you can implement into your real estate business immediately. These strategies will allow you to generate business now.

Zero Cost Lead-Generation Strategies

One of the biggest opportunities for real estate agents today is all of the free and inexpensive lead-generation strategies. Many real estate agents never take advantage of these opportunities. They're always looking to buy the next shiny object or pay for lead generation.

I challenge you to think outside the box and look for every opportunity in your market where there is potential to generate free and inexpensive leads.

Some of the best lead-generation strategies are actually free. One of the best lead-generation strategies is expired leads.

Expired leads are an absolute fundamental strategy for every successful real estate agent's business.

For sale by owner leads are another amazing source of lead generation. For sale by owners are very similar to expireds, in that they have raised their hand and identified themselves as sellers.

Open houses are another amazing and free opportunity to lead generate. Open houses allow you to get face-to-face with homebuyers who are actively out touring homes.

Later in this chapter, we're going to dive deeper with expired lead-generation strategies, for sale by owner lead-generation strategies, and open houses lead-generation strategies, but I'd like to share with you a few other free opportunities where you can generate leads.

These lead-generation opportunities include your email signature. Do you have a traditional email signature or does your email signature have a marketing offer with a call to action?

Think about how many emails you send throughout the day. Is there a compelling offer to buyers and sellers that you can put in front of everyone that you email?

Your voice mail message is also another opportunity to make an offer to buyers and sellers. Think of it as a radio spot. You can direct people to email you or to go to a specific website to take advantage of your offer.

Business cards present another huge opportunity to get your marketing message out to customers. You hand out hundreds of business cards every single year. What if you used your business card like a mini billboard? You can utilize the back of your business card to make a unique offer to customers.

Sign riders and signage offers another opportunity to obtain leads for free. You can capture qualified homebuyer leads that are driving through neighborhoods looking at property by putting unique messages on your sign riders to generate inbound sign calls.

Craigslist is another free marketing opportunity. You can make unique offers to customers searching for real estate. You can create unique messages targeted around a specific geography, targeted around specific sales prices.

This ties back into earlier chapters, where we talked about targeting your ICP and creating unique marketing messages that attract your ideal buyers and sellers. You can promote listings on Craigslist as well.

Your sphere of influence (SOI) and past clients is another free pillar that represents a massive opportunity in your real estate business. These people already know you, like you, and trust you.

The only investment you need to make with this group is an investment of your time to build and maintain these relationships.

By investing in these relationships, you will generate a consistent stream of repeat and referral leads in your business each and every year.

Another free marketing opportunity is property brochures. One of the biggest mistakes I see made by agents is providing too much information on their brochures. I would recommend removing the sales price from your brochure.

This serves two purposes. One, when prices adjust, you don't have to switch out the brochures, which makes your life easier. Two, you can use the back of the brochure to cross-market other listings that you have in the area. You can also use that space to make universal offers.

You can make offers to potential buyers and sellers. You can customize the back of each brochure. You may have a brochure that offers homebuyers access to a free list of other homes in that community or a free list of homes in the same city.

You can also put a seller message on the back of the brochure for homeowners to get a free home evaluation.

Why Expired Leads?

Expired leads may be the number one lead source of every successful real estate agent in the country. Expired leads offer such an amazing opportunity because they're absolutely free and their information is easy to obtain.

Every single day you can run an expired report on your MLS and get access to every home that failed to sell and that came off the market. Many MLS systems offer access to tax records that will provide you with the owner's information.

An advantage to expired leads is that there is a clear motivation and desire to sell their home. They have already attempted to sell their home, which is important because it provides you insight on what they believe their home is worth.

The key to successfully working with expired leads is getting a hold of them first. You have to beat your competition to the customer. In order to be first, you need to know the habits of your competition.

Most agents are trained to start calling expired leads at 8:00am. Because we know that the competition is calling at

8:00am, I recommend getting on the phone at 7:30am.

I know it's early, but it does allow you to reach the expired lead before your competition. If you call too late, you run the risk of reaching an upset homeowner whose phone has been ringing off the hook with real estate agents who are trying to relist their home.

In addition to calling early, you should also call often if you were unable to reach them first thing in the morning. Make at least two to three call attempts on the initial day that the home expired off the market. After that make one call attempt per day for the next week.

Now, once you do reach an expired lead on the phone, you will need to know what to say. You need a good, compelling offer that grabs their attention. This is where having a well-written script is a necessity.

Keep in mind, this person's home failed to sell after many months. They are most likely going to be frustrated with the process and real estate agents so your script needs to quickly build rapport and demonstrate value.

So what do you say? The first thing you need to do is let the person know who you are and why you are calling and then quickly reduce their resistance by saying:

You're probably getting dozens of calls from agents since your home came off the market.

Has that been happening?

We know that this is happening so by asking a question we know the answer to we can transition to the next part of our script which is:

I'm really sorry you're getting harassed by agents like that. I'm sure the agents are telling you how great they are, how many homes they sell, and I bet some are even telling you that they may have a buyer for your home even through they've never seen it. Have you already heard those sales lines?

This part of the script allows us to empathize with the homeowner and set up the next transition which is:

Well, I'm not calling to sell you anything or trying to list your home. As a matter of fact, if you have just a few minutes, I wanted to talk about you and your goals. Why were you even considering selling your home?

This is key in the conversation. This is where you find out where the seller wanted to go when their home was on the market. By finding out where they were going, you uncover their motivation for selling.

After you have uncovered where they wanted to move to,

you move on to their timing by asking when they were hoping to be there by.

These two pieces are critical. They reveal the homeowner's timing and motivation. You can use their timing and motivation as leverage later to get them to reconsider selling their home.

You can ask them, "If you had gotten your home sold yesterday, would you still be moving to (wherever they told you)? Would that still be the plan?"

If they say yes, then you know this person still has a desire to sell their home and move. They're just discouraged and overwhelmed that their home didn't sell.

In addition to uncovering timing and motivation, your script should uncover the challenges or frustrations the homeowner had with the process.

Asking the homeowner why they feel their home didn't sell can give you an insight on what they felt the other agent did wrong or failed to do altogether. When they share this information with you, they are also telling you what they think an agent should do or what type of marketing they think is valuable. This is good insight for when you do set a face-to-face appointment.

At this point you want to ask the homeowner what their

plan is now. They will either tell you that they are interviewing agents to relist the home or that they are holding off on selling their home.

If they say their plans have changed, ask them if they plan on putting their home back on the market in the next year. This will tell you when they want to put the home back on the market.

If they say they are going to relist the home, you need to have a strong, compelling offer for doing business with you and set an appointment. This is where you can use some of the marketing strategies from Chapter 6 to set your services apart from the competition.

Top agents who generate consistent business from expired leads also include direct mail in their marketing strategy to expired leads. Having a two-pronged approach to expired leads where you call them and send them something by mail will increase your conversion rate.

A large percentage of expired leads won't immediately relist their home so having a strategy to market to older expired leads will pay off. I recommend that your mail campaign last at least 12 weeks.

The longer-term marketing strategy is important because none of your competition is going to reach out to these leads after the first few days or week after the home expired. By having a 12-week marketing campaign, you outlast your competition.

The homeowner is no longer getting phone calls or receiving any mailers from your competition. This means your marketing is not competing with a bunch of other agents.

Much older expired leads are also another really good opportunity that you should be taking advantage of. Call expired leads that came off the market 6 months to 18 months ago.

All of this can be done for FREE but it does take a good chunk of time every day. If you want an inexpensive way to take advantage of expired leads in your market, I would recommend that you look into the REDX (http://www.theredx.com).

Their technology ties into your MLS and pulls the expired leads in your market every morning. You can customize what type of homes you want so you are only calling properties that match your ICP. You can select the areas, price range, style of home, and much more.

The system will augment the property address and provide you with the owner's information including any phone numbers associated with the owner. The service is $150 to $300 a month depending on the choice of dialer.

Leveraging a system like REDX will allow you to save significant time every single day. It also allows you to make more outbound calls in less time. You can make 100 to 150 dials per hour. By making more calls, you will reach more clients which will result in you setting more appointments.

BONUS DOWNLOAD
Get access to our list of qualifying questions
http://www.evolverealestatecoaching.com/expired-script

Why For Sale By Owners?

For sale by owners are another great lead source that many successful real estate agents include as part of their lead-generation strategy.

The reason for this is because the leads are FREE, the homeowner has an obvious desire to sell, the leads are easy to get, and the homeowners advertise their contact information which makes reaching them easy.

FSBOs only represent about 8 to 11% of all sales each year. What's important to know is that most of those sales are done between family members or with a personal acquaintance. That means that FSBOs who are marketing their home for sale have an extremely low success rate.

Because they have such a low success rate, FSBOs will eventually seek out the assistance of a Realtor. To have success with FSBOs, you need to get face-to-face with them to build rapport and have a good follow-up sequence so when they give up and look to hire a real estate agent they call you.

Getting Face To Face With A FSBO

Having a well-written script for FSBO leads is an important component in successfully getting face-to-face with FSBO leads. When you call a For Sale by Owner lead, the first thing you want to do is confirm that the home is still available.

Once you confirm the home is available, you want to confirm that the homeowner is willing to work with an agent if they bring a buyer to the property.

Now that you have confirmed the availability of the home and that the owner is willing to pay a commission, you need to get the homeowner talking about the property. You can do that by asking:

Would it be okay if our company included information about your home to our list of qualified buyers?

Okay, great!

Could you tell me a little more about your home?

This script is designed to have the homeowner open up

and talk about their home. After the FSBO finishes talking about their home, it creates the opportunity to ask about their price.

That's great! Sounds like you have a really nice home.

How did you come up with $xxx,xxx as an asking price?

Next, you want to find out where they're going and when they want to be there by. This will give you insight into their timing and motivation. You can use this information and have an approximate idea of when they will seek the help of a real estate professional.

That will lead you to your next set of questions, which are designed to get them to admit that they have not been able to get an offer. Once they say that they have not gotten an offer, you can respond with a surprised sound or tone as if you are shocked that their home has not sold already.

Now you can transition to a state of curiosity and ask them if there is a point at which they may consider interviewing an agent. Many times they will tell you how long they are willing to sell it on their own before hiring a professional.

This next part is a ninja way to set the homeowner up and make hiring an agent the logical next step. You will want to get the seller to negotiate their price. Here is how you do that.

Earlier, you mentioned that you were asking $xxx,xxx for your home. If we had a cash buyer that was looking to close on your timeline, what do you think your bottom dollar would be?

Is $xxx,xxx your bottom line price?

The goal is to get them to negotiate up front and give you their rock bottom price so we can use that in discussion on an appointment.

At this point you are going to set up an appointment to preview the home to see if it matches any of the homebuyers you are already working with. After you set the appointment, you need to ask one last question:

One last thing: If we could show you a way that we could net you more money by working with us in the sale of your home, would you be open to spending a few minutes talking about that when we get together?

When you get face-to-face with the homeowner, you are going to use the information you gather from your phone conversation to make hiring an agent the next logical step.

The homeowner already agreed to pay you a commission if you bring them a buyer. That is half the battle with a FSBO. Next you need to convert the seller's rock bottom into a percentage.

Here is an example.

Asking Price	$200,000
Rock Bottom Price	$194,000
Reduction	$ 6,000

$6,000 / $200,000 = 3\%$ reduction in price

At this point you can demonstrate to the homeowner how they have reduced their net by an amount that is equal to or more than what a real estate professional would charge them and they are doing all the work.

This is your opportunity to now show the homeowner how your service can net them more money.

It should be clear now why having a great script will allow you to gather important information that makes converting FSBOs into listings.

Not all FSBOs are going to agree to list with you on the first appointment so you will need a good follow-up system. New FSBOs have not felt the pain and frustration of not selling their home. They still feel confident in their own ability.

Once they've gone 30, 60, 90 days and have not been able to get an offer, they will become a lot more receptive to hiring a real estate agent, so your follow-up process should include a weekly or biweekly phone call for the next three to four months. So when they are ready to hire a professional, you are who they think of.

One of the best sources I can share with you for FSBO leads is Zillow. Zillow allows For Sale By Owners to list their home for sale on their website. You get the owner's contact information, you can preview the photos of the home, and you can see the features and amenities.

You can also leverage REDX http://www.theredx.com for FSBO leads.

Open Houses

Open houses are another free way for you to generate business. I'm not talking about a traditional open house where you spend two hours in a property, put out three to four signs, wait at the front door for people to show up, and then force people to sign in.

I'm talking about a mega open house. A mega open house is a lead-generation system. You are going to be purposeful about the homes you choose to hold open. The home needs to be in good condition. On a scale of 1 to 10 make sure the home is a 7 or higher and has great curb appeal.

The home should be furnished and at a price point that is aligned to your ICP. You should only hold newly listed homes open.

When you do a mega open house, you need to use 40 to 50 open house signs. These are inexpensive corrugated plastic signs that you can buy for $2 to $3 each.

The signs include a marketing message in addition to the open house arrow. The value we found that works best is a free list of area homes.

The signs are spaced out every couple hundred yards. They will lead customers to your open house.

Once you get the traffic to the open house, the process is much different. We allow people to come into the house and not sit at the front door, which makes it awkward. We set up all of the marketing brochures, property sheets, and the free list of homes in the kitchen.

When clients come in and take the property brochure, we offer them the free list of homes. When they take the free list of homes, you want to tell them that you publish this list of homes every week and it includes vacant, owned homes, and other discounted properties.

Then you need to ask them if they would like to be included and receive access to the weekly list of homes. The offer of discounted properties is usually too good to turn down.

When they say yes, you're going to simply ask them,

"What's the best email address to send it to?" This is step one in capturing the lead's contact information without forcing them to fill out a sign-in sheet.

Once you capture the email address, you then tell them that you can customize their list to their specific wants and needs, if they tell you a little bit about what they're looking for in a home including their price range, features, amenities, location, bedrooms, baths, square feet, and any other specifics that are important to them.

At this point, we've collected an email address and now we know what the buyer is looking for in a home, and now all that's left is getting their phone number.

In order to get a phone number, you need to make an offer that adds value to the buyer. You do that by letting them know that from time to time, you come across incredible deals on homes. You have to use their specific criteria to describe what the deal offers. Here is an example:

> *Now, from time to time I come across incredible deals in Frisco. Homes that are priced below market value because the sellers need to sell quickly. If I came across a home that offered 4 bedrooms, 3 baths, 2-car garage and was 2500 square feet or bigger and it was a steal, what's the fastest way that I can get ahold of you or send you a text?*

The buyer's desire to get a good deal on the home they buy makes this a compelling enough offer that they give you their cell phone. Now you have all the information you need to follow up and convert more open house leads into closings.

What Will These Low-Cost-Lead Generation Strategies Do for Your Business?

Taking full advantage of these free lead-generation strategies will allow you to fill your sales pipeline with now business and future Nurture leads.

These strategies will build your business on a solid foundation and will result in a highly profitable business. You can do all of these on nearly a zero dollar budget.

Doing these activities consistently, will generate two to three closings per month. Once you have a steady flow of cash you can invest in other more expensive lead-generation strategies that generate more inbound leads.

What are Some of the Biggest Mistakes Agents Make When it Comes to Lead Generation?

The biggest mistakes I see agents make is chasing the silver bullet, or magic pill. There's no shortage of lead-generation websites and companies in the market today. They're all trying to extract money from you.

They tell agents that they can generate consistent business

without prospecting, or cold-calling leads. A lot of agents will fall for this. Even though it sounds too good to be true, they still pay these companies. Most of the time it's a waste of money and the leads are poor quality.

Another mistake is that agents don't leverage all the free and inexpensive opportunities first. They don't get all the meat off the bone and squeeze all the juice out of the orange. They jump into more costly marketing opportunities.

Now that we have covered the free and inexpensive lead-generation strategies that you can implement immediately into your business to start generating consistent closings, we will talk about the importance of choosing the right brokerage to support your real estate business.

Chapter 8

WHY CHOOSING THE RIGHT BROKERAGE OR TEAM CAN MAKE ALL THE DIFFERENCE

In this chapter we are going to talk about the importance of choosing the right brokerage or team. We will cover the different types of brokerages and identify the important services and support that you should look for in a brokerage so that you can build a strong foundation and have the ability to grow your business.

Understanding the Different Types of Brokerages

There are three types of real estate brokerages that exist in which an agent can work for. There is the franchise, the independent, and the agent-owned brokerage.

All three types of brokerages have their pros and cons. It's important that you understand some of the pros and cons to each type of brokerage so that you can make the best decision and align yourself with the best option that will allow you to grow your business.

Everyone is familiar with the franchise brokerages. The most recognizable franchises are Keller Williams, RE/MAX, Century 21, Coldwell Banker, Better Homes and Garden, and ERA.

Franchise brokerages offer agents access to basic training, systems, and processes. Some provide these services better than others. Having access to these services can be helpful to newer agents who need more support earlier in their careers.

Franchises also allow agents to leverage their name and reputation to gain the customer's confidence. Agents can lean on the franchise's brand early in their career while they are building their business.

The traditional franchise brokerage is an agent head count model, which means they accept a lot of average agents who each close a few deals a year to make large profits. It's not uncommon for these offices to have 50 to 600 agents in them.

Some of the challenges with franchises are that they can be expensive. They can take 30 to 50% of your commission, which limits an agent's ability to reinvest into their business. The more deals the agent does, the more expensive being with the franchise can become.

There are franchises that offer a cap commission, which is

helpful. A cap is a fixed maximum dollar amount that the franchise will charge you. Once you hit that capped amount, your split can increase up to 100%. The challenge with this is if you decide to grow a team. The capped amount increases based on the number of agents you have on your team, which can make it expensive.

Franchises also have a few other challenges such as limited lead-generation systems for their agents. Most of the time it's the agent's responsibility to invest in lead generation. Franchises also can have cumbersome rules and regulations that hinder your ability to be creative and think outside the box.

Independent brokerage can be anything from a small, mom-and-pop shop, single-agent broker/owner to very large offices with hundreds of agents.

Independent brokerages offer some unique benefits to real estate agents, such as lower fees, higher splits, and more creative freedom.

The challenge to the independent brokerages is that they usually do not have the same level of systems and processes as the major franchises. They usually do not offer any lead-generation systems to their agents. The agent is responsible for everything in exchange for a higher split.

Many times they don't have training and systems to help

develop agents. They are not designed to teach lead-generation or help agents create a brand in the local market.

Often independent brokerages are also based on agent head count where they make their profit from allowing a very large number of real estate agents to hang their license for a small commission split or a fixed fee that recurs monthly.

Some of the challenges can be that the agents who are recruited are lower quality. They allow agents to just hang their license with the broker and do one or two deals a year.

With that said, there are some excellent independent options. It's up to you to ask the right questions to make sure that they offer the level of support you feel you need.

The newest and fastest growing brokerage is a cloud-based agent-owned brokerage.

This brokerage is cloud based, which means it has no brick-and-mortar buildings. This brokerage has little overhead expenses, which allows it to reinvest back into its agents providing agents with stock ownership in the brokerage.

This new brokerage offers a low cap commission that includes a suite of technology including industry-leading platforms for lead generation, contract-to-close software, and much more.

In addition to all of this, they offer their agents a revenue-sharing opportunity for each agent that they attract to the brokerage. This creates a unique passive income opportunity for agents. This has helped many agents create an exit strategy and retirement plan.

Within any brokerage there may also Teams. Joining a team can be very beneficial in the beginning of your real estate career. Usually the team leader is already running a successful business and has systems and process in place which can help agents be successful. They can offer agents lead generation, agent support and training.

No matter which option you choose, you need to make sure that you align yourself with a brokerage that can assist you in achieving your personal goals.

What to Look for When Selecting a Brokerage or Team

When determining which brokerage or team is right for you, you should first identify which areas you need the most support. If you have no sphere or base of customers, a brokerage or team that offers lead generation will be valuable.

If you have a desire to grow a team, you should select a brokerage that is team friendly, a brokerage that will allow you to brand your team and that has low team fees.

If you are a single agent who is doing a lot of production, you should choose a brokerage that offers contract and closing support. This will allow you to spend more time face-to-face with clients and less time managing the paperwork and getting bogged down in low-dollar activities.

Whether you are new or experienced, training is critical in your growth. Your brokerage or team should provide high-level training. This will allow you to ascend from a single agent to a mega team lead.

For newer agents you should align with a brokerage or team that offers mentorship opportunities. This will allow you to shadow a successful, experienced agent who will teach you the ropes and be there to support you as you do your first few transactions.

Commission splits are also important. Aligning with a brokerage or team that has some type of escalating or capped commission gives you the chance to make more money as you grow your business and do more transactions. This will increase your profitability so you can reinvest into your business.

You should also pick a brokerage that will allow you to create your own brand and promote that brand alongside the brokerage's brand. Being able to promote your brand will be essential to become recognized as a go-to agent in the market.

Selecting a brokerage or team that offers additional income opportunities is important because there is no 401K or retirement fund in real estate.

Revenue sharing and stock options are great opportunities to add passive income to your business and build wealth.

What to Watch Out for When Selecting a Brokerage or Team

When you're interviewing different brokerages or team leads, there are a few red flags that you should look out for. Large franchise fees or buy-ins that come along with lengthy contracts are risky. Many times these contracts are one sided. The company can part ways with you for a variety of reasons; however, you are stuck.

Be aware of royalty fees that come off the top of your commission. This is common with many franchises. They take 6% to 8% off the top of your commissions, and there's no cap to that royalty fee. This can become a huge expense totaling $50,000 or more for teams.

Ultimately, each brokerage has its pros and cons. By thinking through what specifically is important to you and having an understanding of what to avoid, you can make the best decision.

Now that we covered the three types of brokerages and reviewed some of the pros and cons for each, you have a better understanding of what to look for when selecting a brokerage. In the next chapter we will go over the step-by-step process to creating a successful strategy plan.

Chapter 9

THE SUCCESS STRATEGY PLAN

In this chapter we will cover the process for building your success strategy plan and review the best ways to create your goals and then reverse engineer those goals into your daily actions.

A Winning Mindset

In order to be successful in anything you do, not just real estate, it starts with your mindset. You have to have a winning mindset. Part of having a winning mindset is to be open minded to the fact that there may be a better way to do business.

A winning mindset includes removing your ego and belief that you have everything figured out and that you don't need help. You need to be open to the fact that there are people, systems, and processes that can help you grow your business much faster.

One of the keys to having the right mindset is being coachable. Personally, coachability is one of the first characteristics that I look for before I consider working with someone. I ask myself, "Is this person open to hearing other potential solutions? Are they willing to trust my recommendations and implement the strategies I lay out for them?"

Agents who have a winning a mindset focus on the positive and how to make things work versus focusing on why things won't work for them. This positive focus is critical because what you focus on grows.

Where you put your energy, effort, and focus will determine the success that you have in all aspects of your life, not just in your real estate business.

Modeling Success

One of the best things you can do is to model success. Modeling allows you to take the guesswork out of your decisions and activities. You can look at other people who have already accomplished what you're trying to accomplish and model them.

Ask Better Questions

I once heard someone say that the quality of your life is in direct proportion to the quality of questions you ask yourself.

If you find yourself consistently asking negative questions, your subconscious mind will answer those negative questions, and you won't like the answers you get.

If you ask yourself good quality questions, your subconscious mind will search for answers that will help guide you to making better decisions.

Here are some quality questions that you can immediately ask yourself that will serve you in a positive way:

"What can I learn from this situation?"

"What could I have done differently?"

These are two great questions that you can use when things don't go as planned. They will allow you to grow from every single opportunity.

Do You Have Smart Goals?

Goal setting is one of the most important things that you can do in your business. To do goal setting properly, your goals need to be SMART. SMART stands for Specific, Measurable, Attainable, Relevant, Time bound. Let's dive deeper into each one of those.

Specific. Specific goals talk about what exactly needs to be accomplished, who's involved in the goals, where it's taking place, and why do I want to accomplish this goal.

Adding specifics to your goal includes putting a number in your goal. An example of this is a specific number of transactions you will do.

Measurable. Measurable goals allow you to answer the question, "How will I know if I've succeeded? How much do I need to change to fit my goal? How many accomplishments or actions will I need to take?"

Measuring the improvement from where you start to where you end will let you know if you've been successful at the end of your next year.

An example of a measurable goal is gross commission income, cash in the bank, or the amount of time you take off. Measuring is important because what's not measured isn't improved.

Attainable. Ask yourself the question, "Do I have the resources needed to achieve this goal? Is this goal a reasonable stretch for me?" You do not want to set yourself up for failure by setting a goal that is not practical based on the current reality.

An example of this in real estate is setting a goal to close

100 transactions in your first year when you do not have lead generation set up, no team and no support. It's impossible to manage 100 transactions while still being able to lead generate and make your prospecting calls. There is not enough time in a day.

Now, setting a goal to close 30 transactions in your first year is a stretch but it's possible.

Here are some questions you can ask yourself to determine attainability. "Are the actions I plan to take likely to bring success? Am I doing the right things to attain the goals I'm setting out towards?"

Relevant. You have to set goals that are important to you, that motivate you, and that energize you. Your goals should be important to you and not just goals that you set because you think they should be important. Your goals should wake you up early and keep you up late at night.

Here are some questions you can ask yourself to make sure your goals are relevant. "Is this a worthwhile goal for me right now? Are my goals meaningful to me or just something others think I should do?"

Time bound. Putting a deadline on reaching your goals is one of the most important aspects of setting good goals. Having a deadline forces you to take action versus procrastinating. A time frame also represents a finish line and something to work towards.

Power of a Written Goal

The absolute most important thing you can do when setting your goals is to write your goals out. I'm going to share with you a research study that was done with a Harvard MBA class on goal setting.

In 1979 a graduating Harvard MBA class was surveyed to determine which students had set goals for themselves. The survey found that 84% of the entire class had set no goals at all. 13% of the class had set written goals but had no concrete plans. 3% of the class had both written goals and a concrete plan.

10 years later this group of Harvard MBA graduates was brought back together to see how each group was preforming in their careers since graduation. The results were staggering. The 13% of the class that had written goals but had no concrete plans were making twice as much money, on average, than the 84% of the class that had no goals at all.

Even more shocking was that the 3% of the class that had both written goals and a plan were making 10 times as much money as the rest of the 97% of the graduating class.

This study clearly shows the importance of not only having

written goals, but also having a plan on how to reach those goals.

Get in the habit of writing your goals each year and taking time to write out what you would need to do in order to achieve your goals. Make sure that you keep your goals in a file and collect them each year so that you can go back over the years and see how far you have come.

People tend to overestimate what they can achieve in one year but dramatically underestimate what they can achieve in 3, 5, or 10 years.

Reverse Engineering Your Way to Success

Let's take your income goal that you have set out to hit this year and reverse engineer your goal back to the key activities that you need to do daily in order to hit your income goal.

The first step in this process is to take your income goals and determine how many transactions you will need to close in order to reach your income. You will first need to know what your average sales price is and what your average income per transaction is. Here is an example:

My Average Closed deal $ 247,500
My Average Commission   x   3%
Commission Per Deal $ 7,425

Now that you know how much your average income per deal is, you divide that into your income goal to find out how many transactions you will need to close to hit your income goal.

Income Goal divided by Commission Per Deal
$150,000 / $7,425 = 20.20 Closed Transactions needed (Round to 20)

Once you know how many closed transactions you need, you can take it a step further and break those transactions down into buyer sides and seller sides. If your business is split evenly between buyers and sellers, you would need to divide your total number of transactions in half.

10 Buyer Closed Transactions needed

10. Listing Closed Transactions needed

The next step is to determine how many listings and buyers you need to work with in order to hit the number of closed transactions you need.

This is where knowing your numbers is important. You

need to know what your taken-to-sold ratio is for both listings and buyers. If you are new or have never tracked this conversion ratio before, you can make an assumption for the first time.

Example:

Listings Sold Ratio = 8 out 10 listings close = 80%
Buyer Closed Ratio = 8 out 10 buyers close = 80%

In order to close 10 listings, you need to take 10/.80 = 12.5 listings taken (Round up to 13)

In order to close 10 buyers, you need to take 10/.80 = 12.5 buyers worked with (Round up to 13)

Now that you know how many buyers and listings you need to hit your goal, the next step will help you get clear on how many appointments you need to go to in order to get 13 listing agreements and 13 buyer representation agreements.

This is called the Met-to-Taken-Ratio. This is where you determine how many people you need to meet with to get a listing agreement or buyer agreement signed.

Example:

Listings Met to Taken Ratio = 7 out of 10 listings close = 70%

Buyers Met to Taken Ratio = 7 out of 10 buyers close = 70%

In order to list 13 homes at a 70% Met to Taken Ratio (13/.70) you need to meet with 19 sellers.

In order to sign 13 buyers at a 70% Met to Taken Ratio (13/.70) you need to meet with 19 buyers.

Now you know exactly how many appointments you need for sellers and buyers throughout the year to hit your goal. Let's take it a step further and break these down to monthly targets.

19 Seller Appointments / 12 months = 1.6 Appointments needed per month (Round up to 2)

19 Buyer Appointments / 12 months = 1.6 Appointments needed per month (Round up to 2)

If your number is bigger, you can break the monthly targets down even further into weekly targets by dividing the monthly targets by 4.

By reverse engineering your BIG income goal down to monthly or weekly small targets, it become less intimidating. Instead of focusing on making $150,000, you can focus on setting two buyer appointments this month.

Smaller bite-size monthly goals allow you to have small victories throughout the process and not feel overwhelmed.

BONUS DOWNLOAD

As a bonus, you can get a free download of my personal action plan that will walk you through the entire process of reverse engineering your goal.

http://www.evolverealestatecoaching.com/personal-action-plan

Additional Tips. Here are a few more conversion metrics that will be helpful for you to track.

You will want to track how many leads you generate.

You will want to track how many leads you reach.

You will want to track how many conversations it takes to set an appointment.

You will want to track your appointment set-to-kept ratio.

Having this level of clarity will allow you to build a predictable model from leads generated to closed transactions. Your business is now running like a machine. If you want to increase your income, you will know exactly how many more leads you need to generate.

Putting Your Plan to Work

Now that you have reverse engineered your income goal down to your monthly and weekly appointment targets, you can align your calendar with your daily activities that it will take to reach your targets.

You have to make sure that you are time blocking the proper activities and giving yourself enough time to hit your targets.

In order to reach your income goal, you need to focus on winning each day and winning each week. If you are hitting your smaller targets along the way, you will be on pace to hit your goal.

Now that you know what you need to do each week, you know how to time block your calendar and you have the conversion skills to turn leads into closings, you need to do one last thing.

You need to take MASSIVE ACTION and start implementing the strategies that I have laid out for you in this book.

CONCLUSION

Now that you know the step-by-step framework for building a predictable real estate business which includes low-cost lead generation strategies, marketing and conversion strategies along with the best time management secrets that will allow you to align your daily activities to achieving your income goals.

You can implement the strategies I have laid out in this book and finally achieve a highly profitable and predictable real estate business that you can enjoy.

In order to help you implement these strategies, I am offering you a **FREE** One-on-One Success Strategy call. These success strategy calls are valued at $647.

During your 60-minute private success strategy call, we will take a deep dive into your business and uncover the following:

- Clarity on what success looks like in your business so that you will know exactly what you are working towards.
- The current challenges in your business that are preventing you from going to the next level which means you will know exactly what to focus on in order to overcome these challenges and take your business to the next level.
- A five-point growth strategy plan that you can use to unlock $50,000 to $100,000 or more in revenue opportunities.

- A predictable model that generates a constant flow of qualified leads so that you never have to worry about when you will get your next commission check.
- How to attract more of your ideal clients which means not having to work with another bad client again.

ARE YOU READY TO TAKE YOUR BUSINESS TO THE NEXT LEVEL?

TO RESERVE YOUR **FREE** SUCCESS STRATEGY SESSION VISIT:

www.EvolveRealEstateCoaching.com/Success-Call

SPOTS ARE LIMITED

Even though this call is FREE, your time is not. If you don't feel that your success strategy call was worth your time, just let me know and I'll donate $250 to your favorite charity.

ABOUT THE AUTHOR

Alexander Piech III

Real estate Trainer & Coach / Strategic Business Advisor / Speaker / Author

Alex Piech began his real estate career in 2003 at the age of 20 years old. He became licensed while attending Western Connecticut State University where he would receive a bachelor's degree in business management.

In 2005 at the age of 22, Alex became one of the youngest RE/MAX franchise owners and opened RE/MAX Preferred Properties in Naugatuck, CT.

It was over the next 10+ years that Alex consistently invested in his personal and business growth. He attended numerous conferences, bought dozens of training programs, received several certifications, and hired two real estate coaches.

During this time Alex became obsessed with learning and understanding what really worked and what didn't. He documented everything and focused on building systems and processes around proven strategies.

Today, Alex continues to invest, develop, and improve his systems. Most recently Alex helped build an innovative real estate brokerage in Frisco, TX where they partnered with local agents and helped them become the dominant go-to listing agent in their market by utilizing unique marketing, lead-generation and conversion strategies. Within the first 12 months the brokerage closed 262 transactions and generated over $2,300,000 in commission income.

Alex's desire is to contribute and help as many agents as possible and show them how to build a highly profitable and predictable real estate business that affords them the ability and freedom to enjoy it. The fulfillment Alex gets in adding value to the lives of others has led him to expand outside of his brokerage and work with agents across the country by offering real estate coaching through his company, Evolve Real Estate Coaching.

Check out more information at

http://www.EvolveRealEstateCoaching.com

www.ingramcontent.com/pod-product-compliance
Lightning Source LLC
Chambersburg PA
CBHW070249230526

45470CB00002B/533